THE
SUPERBABY
SYNDROME

THE
SUPERBABY
SYNDROME

Escaping the Dangers of Hurrying Your Child

BY
JEAN GRASSO FITZPATRICK

HARCOURT BRACE JOVANOVICH, PUBLISHERS
SAN DIEGO   NEW YORK   LONDON

For Matthew and Laura,
who have taught me
so much more than
I could ever teach them.

HBJ

Copyright © 1988 by Jean Grasso Fitzpatrick

Library of Congress Cataloging-in-Publication Data
Fitzpatrick, Jean Grasso.
    The superbaby syndrome: escaping the dangers of hurrying your child / by Jean Grasso
    Fitzpatrick.—1st ed.
       p. cm.
    Includes index.
    ISBN 0-15-186777-1
    1. Child rearing—United States. 2. Child development—United States. 3. Parent and child—United States. I. Title. II. Title: Superbaby syndrome.
HQ769.F525 1988
649'.1— dc1988-11157

Designed by Eileen Boniecka

Printed in the United States of America

First edition

A B C D E

. . . Thou hast hid these things from the wise and prudent, and hast revealed them unto babes . . .

—*Luke 10:21*

Contents

FEW LIFE EXPERIENCES can compare with the amazement we feel as we watch our children discover the world. How eager they are to explore and experiment! And how proud of their fledgling achievements. I'll never forget the way my one-year-old, Laura, claps her hands and smiles to herself after banging out a three- or four-note composition on her red-painted toy piano. Or the day three-year-old Matthew tapped his fingers pensively against the kitchen table for a while and then called out in an excited voice, "Mommy, three and three is six!"

Those are the moments that compensate us for the mountains of diapers we change during the first few years of a child's life, and for the oceans of spilled juice we mop off the kitchen floor. For most parents, it's natural to share children's excitement as they learn. Unfortunately, it's also natural to wish for more excitement and less drudgery! No wonder enrolling in a kiddie gym class instead of going to the supermarket, or setting flashcards instead of Cheerios out on the kitchen table, is so appealing. "I found we got along a lot better when we were out than when we just hung around the house," one mother of a three-year-old told me, "so I signed up my son for a different course every day after nursery school."

Of course, most of us don't get hooked on the superbaby syndrome for reasons of such simple expediency. What parent doesn't genuinely want to help her child develop to his fullest potential? After all, when you think about it, that's a pretty fair definition of our task as parents. But with the superbaby syndrome reaching epidemic proportions, it's getting harder to understand what a child's fullest potential really is, and how it ought to be developed. If you hear enough about ten-month-olds who can tell Bach from Beethoven, and two-year-olds who've learned the alphabet from the TV set, you rapidly begin to lose confidence in your ability to rear your child without assistance from an army of coaches and experts.

That's where this book can help. Like you, I've received hundreds of direct-mail advertisements offering to build my kids' brains through "scientifically" formulated systems, programs, and classes. Like you, I doubted the effectiveness of these products—but I certainly didn't want to risk shortchanging my children. It was hard not to wonder, *Are* kids much more likely to become accomplished musicians if they begin the violin at three? *Is* it easier to learn to read at an early age? *Does* a preschool gym class offer a child opportunities to develop her coordination that she misses climbing trees in the backyard?

As a professional writer specializing in child care and family problems, I decided to use my resources and contacts to find answers to these questions and more. Not satisfied merely with evidence that young children can be trained to exhibit skills that make them appear abnormally sophisticated, I wanted to learn what child-development specialists know about the *long-term* effects of such training. And instead of taking an all-or-nothing approach—either signing them up for the Better Baby Institute or leaving them to cool their heels in a playpen—I wanted to know what I could do to help my kids develop in healthy ways.

All along, my bias has been to follow my instincts and let nature and my children's own inclinations take the lead. I'm happy to report that not only did most of the research I found in academic journals support this approach, but so did my interviews with child-development specialists and experts in various fields, from reading to swimming to computers, and my conversations with numerous parents. Consequently, the chapters that follow aim to present a clear and up-to-date picture of what the experts believe about child development, as well as a guide to understanding what your own child's behavior is telling you from day to day. After all, in the long run, who knows more about your child than you do? And keeping *that* in mind is your best defense against the superbaby syndrome.

Acknowledgments

THAT SO MANY PEOPLE were willing to give generously of their time and expertise for the benefit of this book is a measure of how critical child-development experts and others consider this issue to the future of our children. My deep thanks go to the staff of the information department of the National Association for the Education of Young Children for invaluable help with research; Martha Abbott-Shim of Georgia State University; Louise Bates Ames, cofounder and associate director of the Gesell Institute; Pat Belby, director of the employee child-care center at Little Tikes, Inc.; Margaret Bloodgood, admissions director, the City and Country School, New York City; Brenda Boozer, soprano of the Metropolitan Opera; Barbara Bowman, director of graduate studies at the Erikson Institute in Chicago; Peggy Charren, president of Action for Children's Television; Ann Costello, director of St. Mary's Play School, Scarborough, New York; Kathy Egan, project specialist, and the staff of the American Academy of Pediatrics; Lorraine Fink, editor of *Suzuki World* magazine; Millard Freeman, national director of aquatics for the YMCA of the USA; the folk singer Tom Glazer; my cousin Christopher Grasso of *Education Daily* in Washington, D.C.; Carol Totsky Hammett of Tiny Tot Fitness; Larry Heskett, director of mail-order marketing for the Encyclopaedia Britannica Home Library Service; Catherine Hirsh-Pasek, Ph.D., professor of psychology at Temple University; Charles Hohmann, Ph.D., and Lawrence Schweinhart, Ph.D., of the High/Scope Educational Research Foundation; William Hooks of the Bank Street College of Education Media Group; Ann Jernberg of Theraplay; James Kimble of Kimbo Educational; Stuart Kopperman, M.D.; Marge Kosel, vice president of Sunburst Communications; Lewis Lipsitt, Ph.D., director of the Brown University Child Study Center; Valeria Lovelace, Ph.D., director of research for "Sesame Street"; Lorraine Rocissano, Ph.D.; Irving Segal, distinguished research scientist, and Edward Chittendon, senior research psychologist, of the Educational Testing Service; Professor Sarah Sparrow of the Yale Child Study Center and Yale University School of Medicine; Gordon Shaw, treasurer of the U.S. Association of Independent Gymnastics Clubs and owner of the Richmond Olympiad in Virginia; the Toy Manufacturers of America; Kim Toner of Briarcliff Nursery School; Bretta Weiss, national director of the American Montessori Society; Eleanor Wortley, director of the Suzuki program at the Westchester Conservatory, White Plains, New York; and Edward Zigler, Sterling professor of psychology at Yale University.

Special thanks to Joyce Koyner and the staff of the Ossining Public Library for obtaining books and articles from far and wide, and for extraordinary patience; also to the New York Public Library and the Marymount College Library in Tarrytown, New York.

I would like to thank my editor, Gary Piepenbrink, for his thoughtful reading and constructive criticisms of the manuscript; my agent, Amy Berkower, for her advice and encouragement during a wonderful but hectic year for both of us; Karen Zilversmit of Writers House for many words of wisdom; and the Reverend Paul F. M. Zahl for spiritual guidance. Kari Jahnke, Lori O'Laughlin, Margaret Wallace, and Jane Pachman provided help in countless ways, as did Brooke McKamy Beebe, author of *Tips for Toddlers.* My mother, Jean Grasso, kept me well supplied with clippings and could be counted on for emergency child-care service. And as always my husband, Desmond Fitzpatrick, deserves my deepest thanks for his loving encouragement and support, and for taking over the night feedings so that I could write in the morning—and never once bragging about it.

THE
SUPERBABY
SYNDROME

The Superbaby Syndrome

Unbelievable, but true! Children as young as eight months old can learn math and have fun doing it.

How can I thank you . . . for the many things you have taught me, not only about *How to Teach Your Baby to Read,* but *Teach Your Baby Math.* I think because of you I am a better mother. I'm anxious to start training and developing my son's brain. I've already wasted two years of his life. Send me the math cards quickly. HURRY! Mother waiting.

> A Better Mother
> Honolulu, Hawaii
> —*Direct-mail advertisement for the Better Baby Math Program, $39.95 plus shipping and handling*

"Because I quit my job to stay home with her, I want to devote as much time to her as I can. We've got a whole room dedicated to her books, toys, and blocks, and we change activities every fifteen minutes."

> —*Mother of a two-year-old girl, suburban New York*

Activities for the Third Month
PURPOSE: Smell stimulation.

YOU'LL NEED: Honey, cinnamon, and nutmeg.
TIME: 30 seconds.
BABY'S POSITION: Seated on your lap.
WATCH FOR: Baby's alertness and changing facial expression.

Pass each scent under baby's nose three times. Identify the scents.
—*How to Have a Smarter Baby,* by Susan Ludington, 1985

RAISING A CHILD has never been an easy job, but our generation has managed to make it harder than our grandparents could ever have imagined. Once upon a time toys were fun, kids romped together on the playground, and reading stories was a happy bedtime ritual for parents and children. Now all that's changed. These days "play with purpose" is the name of the game: We carefully select educational playthings to develop our children's eye-hand coordination and visual discrimination. We enroll them in classes where infants train to recognize flashcard portraits of Bach and Beethoven, toddlers learn to swim, and preschoolers do math problems. Hours are spent poring over educational toy catalogs and "working with" our babies on various "developmental playthings." According to a recent magazine article, there are now some 100,000 courses in art, tennis, and swimming available for American preschoolers. Parents from all over the world have used the Glenn Doman method to teach their babies to read, starting as young as six months. Like that favorite of satirists, the couple unable to copulate without consulting *The Joy of Sex,* we seem to have lost a natural ability, the ability to relax and enjoy our children as they grow. How did the benighted offspring of previous generations stumble onto walking and talking with nothing more than mother love (and

Mother Nature) to guide them? It is a paradox that today's so-called superbaby seems to need coaching—complete with exercise videos, baby barbells, and "readiness" toys—just to reach the traditional developmental milestones.

Why has parenting become so complicated? Do our bundles of joy really need all this stimulation before the onset of school-age senility? After all, children have been learning to walk, think, and even read for centuries without being enrolled in baby boot camp. Why are today's parents so worried?

The Selling of the Superbaby

Not long ago I saw an advertisement for a wind-up infant swing in a baby magazine. Reading the copy made me realize I'd been a Bad Parent. Buy this swing, the ad encouraged, and you would give your baby "the healthful motion that's so necessary for good development." Funny, I'd never thought of a baby swing that way. At our house, we've always thought of it as a brain developer for *parents*. How so? Well, when the baby's crying—and when feeding, swaddling, rocking, diaper-changing, pacifying, and every other trick of the parent's trade fail to work—you just pop her into the swing, wind it up, and (seven times out of ten) she'll fall asleep. Which means finally *you* can think straight.

But these days what advertiser would dare suggest a product's main purpose was to lull a baby to sleep? When your child's got kindergarten entrance exams—not to mention the SAT—to prepare for, slumberland is strictly a detour. Right from the start, parents get the message that *stimulation* is the number one task on their job description. Open the "Welcome, Baby" package you receive in the maternity ward, and you find (along with the baby-lotion samples) ads for flashcards, computers, educational toys, and infant exercise routines. And that's only the beginning. Wait till you get home from the hospital and the catalogs start arriving in the mail. One catalog I received advertised an infant bouncer touted as a "Comfort Seat System" ($49.95), featuring an "adjustable Toy Bar" that "brings primary colors, smiling faces, and interesting shapes and sounds to eye level." The manufacturers list further virtues: The bar is "good for early visual stimulation and later, for encouraging reaching and grasping. A unique clip-on system lets you change the toy order and promotes independent play. Each toy was designed by a team of child-development experts." Gone are the days when a few rattles and Mom and Dad's smiling faces were enough to entertain a baby. Toe-tickling and kisses are very nice, thank you, but unless you buy the right educational software you're bound to raise a dull kid. Things have gotten so bad that even canned macaroni is being hawked in magazines as part of the "Chef Boyardee Child Development Series."

Almost every day I open my mailbox to find an advertisement for a new "educational" product or program for my three-year-old or his six-month-old sister: "Your child's coordination, the ease and grace of his or her movements, the sensory-motor skills required for active living are almost completely determined at age 4," warns a baby-gymnastics program brochure. If I don't enroll him, will he turn out to be the Quasimodo of his kindergarten? If I sign her up, will she be the next Mary Lou Retton?

Who knows? Few of us have access to long-term studies specifically confirming or debunking the advertisers' claims. And making a seat-of-the-pants judgment isn't easy for the average two-career couple of the eighties. As adults most of us have had precious little firsthand experience with young children—everyone we knew in college was considerably closer to the drinking age, and no one at the office is under five, either. Furthermore, these days Mom and Aunt Millie don't live next door. As a result, we'll listen to just about any advice we can get. And that makes us the perfect target for pitchmen eager to sell baby-training products and programs. As Michael Schudson puts it in *Advertising, The Uneasy Persuasion* (1984), "Where consumers have personal experience with products or trustworthy secondhand information from friends or school or consumer groups or reliable salespeople, they will be relatively immune to the sales pitch of a commercial. Where these resources are unavailable, they approach the advertisement in greater ignorance and with greater vulnerability." This explains why, when a toy salesperson (who calls herself an educational consultant, no doubt) hands us a glossy catalog filled with pricey playthings and child-psychology jargon, we reach for our wallets. When your first child is a pudgy, leaky bundle of a baby, it's hard to believe she'll ever develop into a grown-up at all (even a klutzy, illiterate grown-up with a tin ear) without an awful lot of help. So when you hear a sales pitch that sounds as though it had been written by T. Berry Brazelton himself, you pay attention. Let's take a look at a typical example.

A Short Course in Baby-Training

The BabyCise Shared Development System is one of several kiddie spinoffs of the adult fitness craze. It was designed by a pediatrician, Dr. Stuart Kopperman, for babies from newborn to eighteen months. According to the sales brochure, "the exercises stimulate the development of the baby's muscle tone, motor skills, and coordination. BabyCise helps build little bodies . . . and that can help build big self-confidence." Products like these can also build the belief that kids can't learn anything without formal training (preferably in the form of a hundred-dollar videotape kit); that parents can only foster baby's development through a standardized program prepackaged by an outside source, something like a Piagetian Big Mac; and, saddest of all, that the spontaneous give-and-take between parent and child— the intimate, playful exchanges out of which fun and games grow so naturally—just isn't enough anymore. Forget everyday adventures like visiting the grocery store together, dancing to the kitchen radio while dinner's simmering on the stove, or chatting and cooing together through diaper changes and baths. Developmentally, they're a washout.

Today's infant needs

- A sixty-minute videotape with "five 10-minute exercise segments, one for each stage of baby's development"

- Two baby barbells ("Each squeaks, rattles, and jingles, and when used with the BabyCise program, helps promote upper torso strength and flexibility.")

- An exercise mat

- Three "Triangle Play Blocks," each of which "encourages baby to crawl and climb, and teaches the meaning of over, under, around, and through"

- A bolster which, "when used with the BabyCise program . . . helps develop upper-body strength and encourages baby's sense of balance" (Presumably, when it's *not* used with the BabyCise program it just sits there being a pillow—like the ones already on your couch.)

What do you do with all this equipment? That depends on which "stage" of BabyCise your child is in. The *newborn* gets away with "gentle stretching exercises and soothing massage" designed to foster "emotional and physical bonding." After that, though, the workout begins. Waiting for your baby to start sitting? "This group of exercises is geared to strengthening the back and trunk muscles needed to hold baby's body upright," promises the brochure. "Coordination and balance are practiced, too." For the still-sedentary infant in the *pre-crawling* stage, the exercises "place special emphasis on the coordination and motor skills that will be used for crawling." Once baby is *crawling,* parents can make sure she will lose no time learning to walk: "Specific exercises geared toward strengthening the lower back and leg muscles will help prepare baby for taking those first exciting steps." Finally, with the baby on her feet, she can start getting ready for the Olympics: the *standing/walking* exercises "improve baby's coordination and balance while helping to build confidence in baby's physical ability."

And why stop there?

If you really want to get serious, you can invest in one or more accessories. There's the thirty-dollar balance beam, for example, that "encourages the stepping reflex in young babies and promotes balance and coordination when used with the BabyCise program."

It's a wonder kids ever learned to walk on the *floor*.

How did Dr. Kopperman, a highly respected member of the American Academy of Pediatrics, end up designing such a product? "I'm not the merchandiser. Matchbox Toys is not me," he says, "and we've had our words about it." Dr. Kopperman explains that he and the original producer of the video initially envisioned a program that would "promote bonding and interaction between parent and child." When the product was picked up by Matchbox Toys, he maintains, "they added some things which they thought would sound good but which were not cleared with me, such as saying that BabyCise may build balance and coordination and strength, and so forth. These were not *my* words. . . . One of the attacks that's been leveled at this program is that we're promising it's going to build muscle tone and balance and coordination, and honestly, *I don't believe that it does.*"

So what *does* BabyCise do?

"A lot of parents work outside the home . . . and they go home and they see this stranger that they haven't seen all day and they want to do something," explains Dr. Kopperman. "And of course they should hug the baby, and they should play with the baby. But some parents—especially in this day and age, when the extended family isn't what it used to be—want to find some time to set aside each day for . . . quality time, time that's just spent for you and the baby, knowing that you're going to spend ten to fifteen minutes every day going through this set routine and seeing progress."

Quality Time and the Training Mentality

In other words, even if baby doesn't need training, Mommy and Daddy do. Packaged baby-training is especially appealing to people who have more money than time. For those of us who have trouble making the transition from the structured workplace to the messy playroom, who might not be inclined to sit down on the floor with a baby and lose ourselves in playful, loving silliness, products like BabyCise offer a step-by-step approach to infant interaction, guaranteed to produce so-called quality time. Dr. Lewis Lipsitt, developer of the Playskool Playtime with Baby program (a similar product that incorporates an audio tape and book) and professor of child study at Brown University, tries to explain: "You can do a lot by having a child play with pots and pans, but parents today are made into better parents by the availability of easy-to-implement products. Somehow having them in a kit facilitates interaction."

"Today's parents are not extremely creative—not because they're not able to be, but because they don't have the time or the energy," echoes the director of the child-development laboratory for a major toy company, requesting anonymity. "When we look at the statistics, we're looking at more than half the parents and children leading very structured lives. But I think that it's on the long days at home—snow days off from school, or rainy days—that the creativity surfaces."

Long, unstructured days were dandy for Huck Finn, but we're used to the goal orientation of the paid workplace—deadlines, schedules, quotas, paychecks, commissions. Our own childhoods spanned the sputnik era, and our days were organized around ballet lessons, Little League, and the Scouts. *New York Times* columnist Anna Quindlen observes, "We are a generation of people who like to play by the numbers: 750 on the verbal SAT, a starting salary of $65,000, two cars. The job of raising children, however, doesn't come with much of a scorecard. A writer has things published, a lawyer wins cases, a doctor saves lives. But it is hard to quantify what a good parent does. Children's achievements tend to be small for a long time—eating with a fork, say, or taking off their own pajamas, or learning to use the toilet."

Whether we continue to work outside the home after our baby's birth or decide to funnel our energies into full-time child-rearing, taking a systematic approach and "seeing progress," as Dr. Kopperman puts it, is not only gratifying but *exactly what we've come to expect.* It's tempting to believe that we can control all the variables in our baby's development and produce the perfect child, just as we can put in overtime on an important project and get a promotion. In the words of an advertising executive who is the mother of a three-year-old girl, "You have career success, good pay, a beautiful home, and what's next? You bring the same approach to raising your child. Only this time it isn't a client or an employer you're dealing with—it's a person's life, so it's that much more urgent." Bring on the eighty-dollar crib mobiles, the two-hundred-dollar playhouses, the thousand-dollar Suzuki programs.

With a program such as BabyCise, which is divided into five "stages" corresponding to baby's development, who can claim to resist looking forward to the next stage? "There's no fixed time-table. You proceed to the next level only when *your* baby is ready," reads the brochure reassuringly. "No frustration. No pressure." Such warnings are included in the advertisements for many early-training programs, but because of the structure of the programs themselves they are often ignored. The children are the losers. I visited an infant gym class run by Playorena, for example, and watched a mother literally push her ten-month-old down slides in an effort to encourage him to crawl—as he screamed in terror each time.

Late but Great

That today's new parents can afford to sink so many dollars into their child's toy chest is evidence of how carefully we plan our families. When we finally decide to abandon birth control and make a baby, it's only after a close scrutiny of our finances and career strategies; that way we can be sure to afford the nursery with all its accoutrements, the right kind of child care and schooling, the "quality time," and everything else the modern baby needs. Once born, this privileged creature ends up with few siblings—what parent feels capable of staging such an extravaganza more than once or twice?—but many playthings and plenty of attention. As a psychiatric social worker who left her job to care for and train her two-year-old daughter said: "This is my project now, I told myself. This is what I'm devoting my life to."

Imagine how much more stimulating the parenting "project" could be if we spent dinnertime discussing the comparative merits of Mozart and Beethoven with our toddlers instead of trying to catch their cups of juice before the next spill! Seeing the parent's job as cerebral conditioning is certainly less depressing than, say, viewing it as an endless procession of runny noses, dirty diapers, and oatmeal stuck to the floor under the high chair. And the entrepreneurs play this for all it's worth. In his book *How to Multiply Your Baby's Intelligence* (1984), Glenn Doman states that the mothers enrolled in his Institutes for the Achievement of Human Potential are learning "to speak Japanese, to read Spanish, to play the violin . . . and to do a host of other splendid things which most women dream of doing." Now instead of trying to get away from their kids, these mothers are learning new skills so that they can teach them. "The guilt at escaping their children had somehow, magically, been transformed into pride and a real sense of high purpose for themselves, their children, and the contributions they would make to the world. These were professional mothers."

It is the rare parent today who admits to being so bogged down in the basics that she has little time for baby brain-building. The only one I met was a mother of three whose twin boys were born when her first son was eighteen months old. "I was just trying to make it day by day," she recalls. "We had sleeping through the night, holding their own bottle, and toilet training to get through. We couldn't worry about computers."

In our devotion to our few, carefully planned progeny, we are not unlike today's parents in China, who are responding to government incentives to limit their family size. According to one report, they are willing to spend a large percentage of their annual pay for fancy toys. As an official of the Shanghai Toy Cooperative Number Two explained to touring American reporters, "Nothing is too good for the one child."

Besides, virtually every writer about childhood, from John Locke to Sigmund Freud, and certainly all the current crop of popular child-care experts (most notably Burton White, author of *The First Three Years of Life,* 1975), has promised that time invested during the preschool years will pay off handsomely in the future. And the baby-training hucksters like Glenn Doman, originator of such programs as *Teach Your Baby Math* (1982) and *How to Teach Your Baby to Read* (1975), do not fail to proclaim, "The *first six years* of life are the *genesis of genius.* . . . It is *easy* to make a baby a genius *before six years* of life."

Now isn't *that* good news! Here's an efficient approach to childhood. Instead of letting your kid waste time pedaling her trike up and down the driveway, invest six short-but-productive years in building her brain. She'll be a genius for life—and you're free to get on with your career. It's especially tempting to see things this way if you've started your family late in the game: When you're in your "prime" and the baby's still in Pampers, sometimes it seems as though you'll be on Medicare before she starts kindergarten. As a result, it's tempting to try to telescope a decade of development into the preschool years. For the generation brought up on instant gratification, why have a child who reads at seven when she could read at three? This attitude contributes to what many writers have called "the disappearance of childhood." Marie Winn observes in *Children Without Childhood* (1983):

> The practical result of early-childhood determinism is a new kind of liberation for parents: if they believe the major part of the human personality is formed before children start

school, once the preschool years are over, parents don't have to worry about how much time they spend with their kids, how much they supervise their activities, how carefully they steer them in one direction or another. They simply have to provide food and clothing, pay the orthodontist's bills, and all will be well.

Unfortunately, as the eminent developmental psychologist Jerome Kagan of Harvard points out in *Infancy: Its Place in Human Development* (1978), there is considerable evidence that the preschool years are not as predictive as is popularly believed. Citing studies that show intelligence tests at the age of three predict IQ and school performance at thirteen, he notes that this "is usually interpreted as indicating that a quality of the child is stable and independent of the continuing environment in which the child is growing." Pointing out that the education and occupation of the child's parents are also correlated with the child's IQ at both ages, Kagan suggests instead that the educational level of a family is the significant factor of continuity, and that "the practices of well-educated parents are such as to produce a high developmental quotient at each age." In other words, if the parents of these children were tuned into their development when they were three, the parents were likely to be equally attuned to their children ten years later.

In support of this interpretation, Kagan cites his own study of a group of ten-year-olds from the Boston area who had been extensively evaluated four times during the first three years of life for attentiveness as well as for several other factors. Comparing the early findings with the children's later scores on intelligence and reading tests, Kagan found that "the educational level of the family was the best predictor of both IQ and reading skill"—rather than early indications of attentiveness. Kagan concluded that his data did nothing to support the theory that the experiences of the first two years set a child on a course that will persist through life. In fact, he warns, the study "does imply that if the structures created by those early encounters are not supported by the child's current environment one should be prepared to see dramatic changes."

Why are so many of us willing to believe that personality and intelligence are graven in stone before a child starts kindergarten? According to Kagan, it is because "a particular recipe of interactions is still seen as an elixir young children need to obtain society's highly valued prizes." In a culture where human worth is measured in terms of career success and material wealth, swiping at a crib mobile amounts to baby's first attempt at reaching for the brass ring. And in a society where the pursuit of upward mobility is not merely an option but an obligation, the ability to *control* one's future, and that of one's children, becomes all-important. When we buy into this value system it's no surprise that—like the father in an insurance-company commercial who gazes proudly at his infant daughter and says in a choked-up voice, "She's gonna go to Yale"—we feel we're duty-bound to set them on the fast track right from the start.

What Do *You* Know About Parenting, Anyway?

It is a serious question in my mind whether there should be individual homes for children—or even whether children should know their own parents at all. There are undoubtedly much more scientific ways of bringing up children, which will probably mean finer and happier children.
—B. Watson, *Psychological Care of the Infant and Child*
(1928)

In pursuit of that "particular recipe" mentioned by Kagan, the experts have been trying to teach us how to raise our kids scientifically, and even get rid of us, for a long time now. Shortly after the turn of the century, when the saying "Early ripe, early rot" was on everybody's lips, parents were warned against playing with their young infants at all to avoid overstimulating them and thereby interfering with their natural growth and development. Now we've gone to the other extreme. Today, as child-development experts tell us more and more about how children learn, who can resist trying to help her child along? "Once people thought newborns couldn't see for three weeks, and of course, that was wrong," says Dr. Lipsitt. "I think what has happened is that as parents have come to appreciate that their children have more talents than they were given to believe—mostly by pediatrics writers of forty years ago—they have begun to try to capitalize on those talents, if they can, to promote learning."

Harmless enough in theory, and maybe even desirable—except for the fact that so many parents find that once they're involved in an early-learning program, they begin to doubt their competence to understand their own child in the face of advice from "authority" and the pressure from other parents in the group. The parent who tries hardest to read her child's personality, to be sensitive to her child's own peculiar needs and inclinations, is bound to find that no single method ever really "works" perfectly for her child, since the process of learning is considerably more complex than, say, programming a computer. To stand by your belief that the most popular early-learning program in town is wrong for your child takes more confidence than many new parents have. Who needs the pressure?

And if the peer pressure doesn't get you, the scary prospect of your child's unknown future will. How can you know now whether you're making a mistake by not buying software for your three-year-old? Will she be unemployable in the year 2006? In the shorter term, if you don't crack those preschool workbooks, will she be the only illiterate in her kindergarten class?

"I'm not into teaching my kids the alphabet because it seems like a boring way to interact with them," a mother of two preschool boys told me. "But I went through a period of sitting down with my son in front of 'Sesame Street' so he could learn his letters. If that's going to be expected of him, I guess we'd better do it. From what I hear, so many kids come to kindergarten reading that the norms have changed."

The message that Mom is to blame for any failure of product or program comes across loud and clear: "Take your phone off the hook and put a sign on your front door that reads Silence—Professional Mother at Work—Do Not Disturb," recommends a chapter of Doman's *How to Multiply Your Baby's Intelligence* entitled "How to Create Success for Your Child." "If you have a quiet, unenthusiastic voice, change it. Create enthusiasm in your voice, and your child will absorb it from you like a sponge. . . . A highly organized mother has a strong sense of purpose about what she is doing. She knows exactly what she has done, how many times she has done it, and when it is time to move on. . . . Very fine professional mothers sometimes fall by the wayside only because they never take the time to sit down and get themselves organized."

Knowing the way your child likes his sandwich cut at lunchtime and offering a hug and a Band-Aid at the right moment may once have been enough to make a good Mom, but today we all seem to need a crash course in Piagetian development before we are allowed to feel competent. You can hardly buy a simple toy anymore without being assaulted by jargon. In the Discovery Toys catalog, for example, every product is labeled for "educational play value": A set of nesting cups, for example, develop "pre-reading and math skills, color identification."

Likewise, in the blitz of manuals telling us how our children develop—over four hundred, according to the current *Books in Print*—we are too often subjected to the kind of advice offered in Genevieve Painter's *Teach Your Baby* (1982). To turn your twenty-nine-month-old into a whiz kid, says Painter, "Each day you could select the activities for a program so that they include at least one activity from each category of training—fine motor, gross motor, problem-solving, language, etc."

Now *really*. Even without Mom or Dad selecting his activities, the average untutored preschooler gets most of this "training" before he's finished breakfast. At least my son does. He carefully picks the raisins out of his cereal and eats them one by one, discarding the bran flakes (fine motor). Then, disgruntled because his banana from last week's shopping trip has a black mushy spot on it, he climbs on a stool to reach the new bananas in the fruit basket on the counter (problem-solving). Or he tries to persuade me that ice pops are the perfect breakfast food (language).

As for gross motor activity, what two-year-old needs to be coaxed into *that?*

When all of growing up is reduced to the acquisition of cognitive and manipulative skills, child development becomes a peculiarly formal process that would no doubt be more efficient if it occurred in a laboratory rather than a messy place like home. And we begin to think our kids would be much better off if psychologists were raising them instead of us. This discounts so many important, real-world lessons parents teach their children. The *real* kids I know have to learn to sleep through the night, eat solids, stop interrupting, dress themselves, knock before opening doors, say "Please" and "Thank you," share their toys, be kind to their siblings, and on and on. Even more important, they need assurance that they are worthwhile people, that their own dreams and imaginings are valuable, and that they have the power to explore anything that captures their curiosity.

Brilliance or Burnout?

> "If we're waiting in the doctor's office or in line somewhere, I try to get her thinking, rather than just sitting there letting our minds do nothing. So I drill her any time we have the chance—letters, numbers, parts of the body."
> —*Mother of a three-and-a-half-year-old*

Even though, as Dr. Lipsitt says flatly, "there are a lot of things we don't know and we're talking ourselves way ahead of the game," it's tempting to think of early training as an insurance policy. Why not go ahead with a training program anyway, on the grounds that it certainly can't do any harm? Mainly because there's plenty of evidence to show that learning to spout a quick response to a flashcard is not only of dubious educational value to your child but also likely to *hinder* the development of other qualities that do bring children lifelong satisfaction and success on their own terms: qualities such as self-esteem, a sense of mastery over their environment, and the tenacity to see a task through to completion. Overload your child with formal, pro-grammed activities and you're likely to end up with a victim of baby burnout. As Edward Zigler, Yale University psychologist and former director of the U.S. Office of Child Development, told me, "Too many kids are . . . getting a message that says, 'You'll love me if I accomplish, if I achieve, if I win.' That's destructive to the child's sense of self-worth."

Such a child is highly unlikely to produce the achievements so devoutly wished for by her parents. "One of the bad effects of parents' getting too involved too early is that they destroy the child's sense of initiative and autonomy," says the psychologist David Elkind of Tufts University, former president of the Na-tional Association for the Education of Young Children and author of *The Hurried Child* (1981). "The problem is that these kids become overdependent on adult direction and guidance."

Reading about the lives of the Quiz Kids, a group of prodigies whose radio program was a national obsession during the 1940s, in Ruth Duskin Feldman's *Whatever Happened to the Quiz Kids?* (1982) makes it very clear that brains and knowledge alone do not guarantee success or happiness in adult life. As Feldman, herself an original Quiz Kid, puts it, "the top achievers were those who, from childhood on, evinced noticeable drive, ambi-tion, initiative, independence, and persistence. Those who *chose* a vocation rather than drifting into one." In the real world, quick answers to hard questions aren't enough, notes Feldman. "In a sense, our easy Quiz Kid acclaim gave us a false view of the world. Those of us who were most celebrated on the show, especially if we started very young, grew up with the impression that we could be winners just by knowing the right answers, being cute and modest, raising our hands, and waiting to be called on. But adult society does not automatically reward the quick, the bright, the artistic. Indeed, society does not automati-cally reward anybody—something some 'smart' people never learn. Adults, unlike children, rarely get ahead except on their own initiative, nor profit save by their own effort."

Some of the children on the program grew up to consider their early achievements as something of an albatross. Quiz Kid Richard Williams, who at age ten could play the *Moonlight Sonata* while working complex algebra problems, is a case in point. He learned to read at age three, starting with his alphabet blocks, and in nursery school liked to read fairy tales to the other children. Considered the brightest of all the Quiz Kids, Williams chose to enter the Foreign Service. In Feldman's book, he explains why, in his own eyes, he had not risen far enough in his chosen career. On the radio program, he says, "the path was laid out for you. It was made clear in what way you had to be assertive. You were not left to find it out for yourself. I think that, as a result of the set of mind induced by 'Quiz Kids,' when, afterward, you did not get automatic recognition for work well done, the disappointment was great . . ." Making it in the adult world required not only the cognitive skills that create a so-called superbaby, but the interpersonal ones learned on the playground and in the ball field. To make matters worse, Williams seemed to find himself continually failing to live up to his original great expectations. Ultimately, he wrote in a letter to Feldman, "the Quiz Kids experience seems to have produced in me standards of success so high as to constitute a difficulty, making adult attainments which for most people might be amply fulfilling seem less than fully sufficient."

Quiz Kid Joel Kupperman, a math whiz on the program, was even more disillusioned. At his audition, asked to multiply twenty-four by ninety-eight, the five-year-old had shot back, "Dat would be two thousand three hundred fifty-two." According to the *New Yorker*, his father, an engineer who enjoyed math, "first realized he had a fellow mathematician in the family when he saw that his infant son, instead of chewing the beads on the side of his crib, was using them as an abacus." At the age of four, he could total his mother's grocery bill faster than an adding machine, says Feldman, and once caught the grocer shortchanging her.

After ten years on the "Quiz Kids" program, however, Kupperman came to disparage his achievements as mere "calculator's tricks" and decided to study philosophy, in part, he said, because of his dissatisfaction with the "fast, superficial answers" featured on the show.

In Feldman's book there is a page of excerpts from Quiz Kids' advice to parents of gifted children. While many of these kids showed early promise without any unnatural training by their parents, many did feel they'd suffered the consequences of too much parental enthusiasm. One piece of advice offers a graphic warning against succumbing to the superbaby syndrome: "Provide multiple opportunities, but don't push," said one Quiz Kid. "Offer a cafeteria, not a stomach tube."

Healthy Learning

"I give her all sorts of dress-up clothes, help her play out her fantasies, and organize pretend mailings of presents at Christmas. We visit orchards and cider mills together. I have no idea what my daughter will gain from all this, but it seems to me that if you have enough self-esteem, and you know how to learn, you're going to make it in life. I want to *empower* her. I worked at a shelter for battered women for two years, and the women who end up being battered feel helpless. They're victims. Bethany knows she can influence her environment."

—*Psychologist and mother of a three-year-old*

Deciding that you're not going to get sucked into the superbaby machine does *not* mean you have nothing positive to contribute to your child's growth. On the contrary, by refusing to buy into a mass-market vision of cognitive development you are committing yourself as a parent to using your own brain to foster your child's growth as an individual. Unlike the parent who relies on a commercial tape, computer program, course, or manual, your tools are your ability to understand your child and your imagination, sensitivity, and warmth.

In their book *Cradles of Eminence* (1962), psychologist Victor Goertzel and Mildred G. Goertzel analyze the childhoods of over four hundred famous twentieth-century men and women. Their conclusions leave no doubt that behind most adult high achievers is at least one *highly involved, but not pushy, parent.* "In homes which cradle eminence there are strong tendencies to build directly on personal strengths, talents, and aims," they write, "rather than to assume that there is a large, specific body of knowledge that everyone should possess." So much for the "gourmet baby" who is trained to become an expert in every field of endeavor. "There is a personal involvement with ideas in these homes," conclude the Goertzels. "There are few passive receptors of fact." So much for flashcards.

The Goertzels also emphasize the importance of profound and spontaneous sensory experiences in a child's life (not to be confused with the contrived exercises recommended in *How to Have a Smarter Baby*). These moments of overwhelming self-discovery are exactly the opposite of the two-dimensional, pencil-and-paper approach to early learning taken in workbooks. "In several of the four hundred can be found an exceptionally keen response to sensory stimuli which set them apart from others." They tell how the philosopher and physician Albert Schweitzer almost fainted the first time he heard brass instruments played in harmony, how the artist Salvador Dalí took pains to describe himself as a person reacting to sensations rather than ideas or words, and how the architect Frank Lloyd Wright remembered the colored papers and wooden blocks his mother gave him as his first toys. If our children spend all day with classes, drills, and other forms of structured learning, when will they have time for these kinds of seminal experiences?

As Ann Jernberg, director of Chicago's Therapy Institute, sees it, there are many healthy ways for a parent to help a child learn.

"What's important? Dinner table conversation, books, and magazines," she says. "If your child gets excited about robins and blossoms on a tree outside on a spring morning and you go from there—show him pictures of birds, or go to an aviary—that's following the child's lead." This is the kind of involvement with children's learning that will help their self-esteem and curiosity about the world around them grow along with their knowledge of isolated facts and skills—and that will *keep them learning.* "If you have just twenty minutes, in those twenty minutes you can make the child say, 'Boy, am I special,'" says Jernberg. "Make your child feel important in his own right. Make him feel every day is a birthday."

For the child whose parents get sucked into the superbaby syndrome, every day is a *work*day. When we succumb to the desire to *control* our children's development rather than to encourage their natural curiosity and enthusiasm for learning, everyone is the worse for it. Our children are deprived of the opportunity to develop the creativity, problem-solving skills, and self-esteem that come with learning and exploring on their own initiative without worrying that their worth depends on how well they perform. At the same time parents end up spending vast sums of money and effort on programs and products of dubious value—not to mention constantly feeling anxious that there's always one more course and one more educational toy out there that their kid is missing. Obviously, this situation does little to foster a healthy, loving relationship between parent and child.

But although encouraging a child's natural curiosity—"following the child's lead," as Ann Jernberg suggests—is undoubtedly a more sensible approach, it's easier said than done. One reason the early-training programs have become so popular is simply that they're available, well advertised, and easy to use. You pay your money and you know your child is getting something that at least *somebody* thinks is valuable. Sitting at home around the kitchen table, it's hard to pin down exactly what your child is learning, if anything at all.

In the chapters that follow, you'll find some answers to your questions. You'll learn exactly how much child-development experts know (and don't know) about the way preschoolers learn from reading, music, movement, computers, television, and the rest of their world. You'll also find out how to help your child learn in healthy and developmentally appropriate ways, without pushing or pressuring. Not only will you be promoting her intellectual development, but you'll be helping her develop a healthy self-esteem that will stay with her all through life.

First Step to Superbabyhood: The Testing Treadmill

"After Ben's physical, I asked the pediatrician, 'Tell me, doctor, do you think he's bright?' "

—Mother of a fourteen-month-old

"I can hardly wait until Lisa starts school so the teacher can tell me how smart she is."

—Mother of a two-and-a-half-year-old

As a modern parent, you are interested in more than feeding and diapering your baby. You want to know your child's potential—so you can start developing it as soon as possible.

Test Your Baby's I.Q. offers an easy and interesting way to find out how advanced your child is for his or her age, and sets your child on the right track to success—now.

—*Back cover,* by Marcia Rosen, *Test Your Baby's I.Q.,*
1986

> Two mothers walking in the park, babies in strollers. One turns to the other: "How are his scores?"
>
> —*New Yorker* cartoon

IT'S SO HARD for new parents not to get sucked in. Only seconds after your baby draws his first breath and the cord is cut, he's taking his first test. Our mothers may have contented themselves with counting five fingers and toes on each hand and foot, but *we* listen for the Apgar score summing up heart rate, breathing, muscle tone, reflexes, and color. By rating our newborn's ability to successfully endure the process of birth, how much this score seems to prove about his ability to meet the challenges that await him in the future (not to mention our own ability to produce a perfect child)!

The pattern of testing, testing, testing continues with the twice-a-month visits to the pediatrician, where we provide detailed accountings of baby's latest "milestones." The anxiety of this can often force us into making ludicrous efforts to ensure the milestones are reached. One mother confessed to me that knowing the doctor was going to ask, "Is she walking yet?" at the twelve-month checkup made it hard to resist giving baby a few extra practice strolls up and down the hall in the last few days before the appointment, just to help her along. Not to mention buying her a pair of shoes "for support." And when we're feeling particularly anxious *between* office visits we can gauge baby's progress ourselves, of course, by opening virtually any child-care manual and turning to the development chart. If we're doing a really good job, baby will be swiping and grasping and sitting and standing light-years (or at least weeks) ahead of the norm.

And why shouldn't we be anxious? Aren't we forever hearing from experts that the intelligence of a lifetime develops in a child before he even learns to pee in the potty? After all, in most child-care manuals, the early years are broken down into a series of three-month stages, with children apparently progressing from one to the next in lockstep. To the uninitiated, it looks as though the slow starter will never finish the race. As Jane Healey asks rhetorically in *Your Child's Growing Mind* (1987), "If the train is late, will we miss the boat?"

Now, some of the authors of these charts do try to be reassuring, but what parent really believes them? Do *you* pay any attention when Frank and Theresa Caplan warn in *The First Twelve Months of Life* (1978), *"Please* do not regard this chart as a rigid timetable. Babies are unpredictable. Some perform an activity earlier or later than the chart indicates." Of course not. If your baby is slow to sit up or walk, surely that's a potential danger sign? Could there be something wrong with him? Or maybe he's just not all that bright?

In fact, most of us are far more likely to fall for the likes of the handy quizzes in Marcia Rosen's *Test Your Baby's I.Q.* Try these on your one-month-old, for example: "Can your child be quieted by a familiar, friendly voice?" "Will your child quiet down when picked up?" Obviously, personality, developmental maturity, and even your baby's digestive system have at least as much to do with the answers as his intelligence does, but what parent can really accept that in her heart of hearts? If your newborn happens to be colicky, you might be left with the impression that baby is not only cranky but stupid as well.

Unfortunately, when you measure your baby's worth against every yardstick that comes along, you're undermining one of your basic functions as a parent, that of being your baby's number-one fan. This is how the testing mentality makes its pernicious contribution to the superbaby syndrome. From the very first developmental-milestone chart you use to check your child's progress and find out what he should be doing next, the tests serve as an encouragement to turn childhood into a horserace, with the emphasis on beating everyone to the finish line rather than responding to what makes your child unique and special. If you let your interactions with your kids become practice sessions designed to keep them up with the charts, you're depriving them—and yourself—of what makes the relationship between a parent and child most satisfying. No one but you is as deeply excited and touched by your child's unique strengths. No one but you shares his joy in discovering his world in quite the same way. No one but you has the opportunity to offer the unconditional love and support a child needs in order to develop self-esteem—the self-esteem that will do much more to help him grow into a healthy adult than any early-training program designed to raise a test score. "I would not say parents need to evaluate their own children," Dr. Martha Abbott-Shim of Georgia State University told me in an interview. "I think we need to support, encourage, and facilitate our children's development—we don't need to evaluate them."

The rest of the world, though, seems to think children do need to be evaluated. At every opportunity. Nursery schools and kindergartens perform screenings, administer developmental tests, and (in the case of big-city private schools) may even require your three-year-old to take a preschool counterpart to the SAT known as the ERBs. That's why now is the time to look at two basic points: why we as parents so easily buy into the testing mentality, and what the tests can and *can't* tell us about our child.

Let's begin with the first: why *are* we so ready to accept what standardized tests and quizzes tell us about our kids rather than what we ourselves can observe in the course of our daily lives together? Well, for one thing, we're the generation that grew up on standardized tests. *We* can read the writing on the wall. Like it or not, test scores cast a long shadow over our lives: As we all know, lots of teenagers score below seven hundred on the SAT, but *they* aren't the ones who are going to make it to Harvard. So your baby sucked his toes at seven months instead of five? *He'll* never drive a Volvo. If you expect to make it in our society, you have to know how to play the game—which means being in the right place (or stage of development) at the right time. Suggesting that a child's future happiness and inner peace may not depend on reaching these goals seems naïve; and when success and achievement are so greatly prized, most parents feel called upon to help their children learn to compete—if only for the sake of survival in the big, bad world.

But fortunately here in the land of opportunity, just about

anything can be made bigger and better, including a baby's brain. So when your newborn seems to be lagging behind, you just start him on a remedial program. Turn to the second section of *Test Your Baby's I.Q.,* entitled—you guessed it!—"How to Improve Your Child's Performance." Or try the Denver Developmental Activities produced by the people who put out the widely used Denver Developmental Screening Test, described in the catalog as a "series of activities arranged by chronological age for mothers and other caretakers to undertake with children aged birth to six years. The activities are designed to help young children develop basic skills in four main areas: large muscle development; small muscle development; speech and language; and personal social skills." What this and other programs do, in the process, is play to today's parents' well-developed anxiety about their kids.

Do we really need to be so anxious? How much do all the charts and tests mean in the long run? What if your baby *doesn't* leap from milestone to milestone with lightning speed during those first three years? Is it true, as the well-known child psychologist Burton White would have it, that the first three years of life are the make-or-break period in a child's development?

Not necessarily. In fact, many child-development experts vigorously disagree with White and even speculate that his claims for the importance of the early years were exaggerated in order to gain financial support for his research on early education for deprived children. As one wag put it, the first three years *are* very important. For that matter, the *next* three years are very important. As are the next three, and so on.

By emphasizing that much could be done to foster a child's development during the first three years, White was part of a general movement during the 1960s and 1970s reacting against the widespread notion that intelligence was strictly *genetic* and *fixed*—something you were born with that could never change, like blue eyes. This was an old notion, one that gave little hope to underachieving children from deprived backgrounds. It was succinctly expressed in *How the Mind Works,* by C. Burt and others (1934): "By intelligence, the psychologist understands inborn, all-round, intellectual ability. It is inherited, or at least innate, not due to teaching or training . . . Fortunately, it can be measured with accuracy and ease." Today the pendulum has swung the other way. Unfortunately, though, it seems to have swung too far. Many entrepreneurs in the early-training business are now trying to persuade us that any kid can become an Einstein, as long as we start teaching early enough.

This controversy over the predominance of environment or heredity has filled one academic journal after another. But do we need to go to these journals for guidance? As parents, we have the privilege of relying on our own common sense when we care to do so, and this is one instance in which that seems like a prudent approach. You're undoubtedly aware that certain types of interaction with your child at certain stages—a game of catch, reading a story, cuddling in an overstuffed chair—can do a great deal to foster his development because they are the right thing at the right time. The growth of intelligence, in other words, seems to depend on an interaction between the child's inherited abilities and the world he is coming to know. And in fact, although their points of view are often oversimplified in the popular press, some of the world's greatest thinkers on child development have offered just such a commonsense model.

Perhaps the most important exponent of this model is the Swiss philosopher and psychologist Jean Piaget, whose studies of children's cognitive development are so often quoted—and distorted—in articles, books, and toy advertisements today. Two of his early books, *The Origins of Intelligence in Children* (1936) and *The Construction of Reality in the Child* (1937), offer remarkable insights into the way children learn. Unfortunately, they're as complex as they are fascinating, which is probably why they're so often misinterpreted. Popularized versions of Piaget often give the impression that you can train your child through each Piagetian stage, more or less the way you'd have a circus lion jumping through hoops. But Piaget stood firm against any such interpretation of his work. In reality, rather than adding his voice to the debate over whether intelligence is a function of heredity or the environment, he suggested a third alternative—one that is far more complex and requires far longer explanation than can be offered in a toy-catalog blurb. Drawing on his training as a biologist and closely observing his own children, Piaget sought to show that cognitive growth occurs through constant *interplay* between the child at a particular level of neurological development and the objects, people, and events in the world around him that allow him to practice skills corresponding to that particular level of development.

In Piaget's view, children exhibit different *kinds* of intelligence at each stage of life, and during each period, they practice these skills by interacting with the environment. During the *sensorimotor* period, from birth to twenty-four months, for example, a child begins to understand that objects exist even when hidden from sight (like a ball under a blanket), ideas such as cause and effect (when I kick the mobile, the balls rattle), and that various means can be used to attain goals (standing on a chair makes it possible to reach the cookie jar). Piaget calls each bit of understanding or knowledge a *schema,* and the schemata (schemas) combine to form a scaffolding of thought on which the child fits new information from the environment.

As Piaget saw it, the child can only come to understand, or *assimilate,* an object in the environment in accordance with his period of mental development. Thus, to be of use, the stimuli must be appropriate to the schemata. In other words, if your baby is just beginning to work on the idea that he can put an object into a cup, offering him a map-of-the-world puzzle will do little to develop his intelligence (unless he decides to plop Iceland and Zambia into the cup).

Unfortunately, although Piaget's contributions to our understanding of children have been undeniably great, they are limited to one aspect of development, the cognitive sphere. Piaget was intrigued with children's perceptions—whether they see a tall, thin glass of water as holding more than a short, fat glass, for example, or whether they think ten blocks spread over a large space amount to more blocks than the same number stacked in a small pile. In short, Piaget was concerned almost exclusively with intellectual functions.

"He was not a practical psychologist. Piaget was studying how we acquire knowledge," observes Dr. Irving Segal, distinguished research scientist at the Educational Testing Service in Princeton, New Jersey. "We've learned a lot from him in certain ways. But he admittedly did not focus on a lot of other things. Piaget was *never* interested in individual differences—why children develop differently. And he minimized the importance of emotions in development."

In *Frames of Mind* (1981), Howard Gardner writes, "While the broad outlines of development as sketched by Piaget remain of interest, many of the specific details are simply not correct." Pointing out that human cognitive development is far more uneven and piecemeal than Piaget's stages suggest, Gardner goes on to say that "rather than a whole series of abilities coalescing at about the same time (as Piaget would have it), theoretically related abilities turn out to emerge at disparate points in time. . . . Piaget's scheme may well be the best that we have, but its deficiencies are becoming all too evident."

IQ Versus Intelligence

Gardner's criticisms reflect his position in the vanguard of the contemporary movement to redefine intelligence as something that has many aspects. Cognitive thinking, according to this view, is merely one of these aspects. But, as Gardner points out, we use the word *intelligence* so often that it seems "we have come to believe in its existence as a genuine, tangible, measurable entity, rather than as a convenient way of labeling some phenomena that may (but may well not) exist." In attempting to define intelligence, he says that it "must entail a set of skills of problem solving, enabling the individual to *resolve genuine problems or difficulties* that he or she encounters and, when appropriate, to create an effective product—and must also entail the potential for *finding or creating problems*—thereby laying the groundwork for the acquisition of new knowledge.'' Instead of accepting the idea of one abstract, all-purpose intelligence based on cognitive thinking, Gardner proposes a theory of ''multiple intelligences,'' noting that ''in the normal course of events, the intelligences actually interact with, and build upon, one another from the beginning of life.'' He calls these intelligences ''frames of mind,'' and outlines six of them: the linguistic, musical, logical-mathematical, spatial, bodily-kinesthetic, and personal intelligences.

Robert Sternberg, a professor of psychology at Yale, suggests another theory of intelligence based on what he perceives as three very different ways of thinking in the human brain. He identifies one of these ways as ''componential'' intelligence, which enables the kind of analytical thinking we're usually referring to when we say someone is ''intelligent.'' But he also describes two other forms of intelligence—''experiential,'' which includes the ability to think creatively and to combine experiences with fresh insights; and ''contextual,'' which is more or less ''street smarts.''

What do all these theories mean to the anxious parent of a young child? Well, they suggest an approach to evaluating our kids that more fully appreciates their unique talents and inclinations, rather than just branding them ''very bright'' or (perish the thought!) ''not particularly bright.'' When you single out what Gardner calls ''logical-mathematical'' intelligence, or Sternberg terms ''componential'' intelligence—and when you see a test score as the sum total of your child's achievements and lifetime potential—you're blinding yourself to the full range of his abilities. Perhaps his special gifts, or ''intellectual propensities,'' as Gardner calls them, lie in other kinds of intelligence. ''I wish my daughter would apply herself more in nursery school,'' one mother of a three-year-old grumbled to me. ''The teacher says she talks too much.'' Perhaps this child is well endowed with linguistic or personal intelligence, to use Gardner's terms, rather than being the goof-off implied by the teacher's remark. As your child progresses through school and enters the adult worlds of family and work, he will draw on a much wider range of talents than his cognitive intelligence in order to function successfully. But that should be obvious. After all, does *your* boss have an IQ of 160?

Testing the Tests

This brings us to the second basic point brought up earlier in this chapter: what the tests can and *can't* tell you about your child. Realizing that intelligence is so hard to pin down should let you breathe a sigh of relief if you've been worried that a preschooler—or any person—could be summed up in a three-digit number or percentile score. It should also help to know that few of the tests for preschoolers even *claim* to be concerned with intelligence per se. What they do aim to tell is whether a child's development is progressing within a normal range at a particular point, and what types of educational experiences will be most beneficial to him at that time.

Although testing was originally intended as an aid in education, it's no secret that too often it becomes an end in itself. The superbaby syndrome is a by-product of this way of thinking. Where young children are concerned, many early-childhood experts worry that the easy availability of development charts encourages parents to force babies through their paces to meet the schedule. "If he'd only stop standing on his toes, he'd have no trouble walking," the mother of a twelve-month-old told me as she brought her son out into the middle of her living room and let go of his hands, apparently hoping to surprise him into standing alone. (He promptly fell onto his diapered bottom, needless to say.) Yet it's a very easy trap to fall into. No matter how many experts tell you that comprehension is an essential part of reading, and that you can help your child develop that ability simply by reading aloud on a regular basis, don't you sometimes wonder whether you should drill him in the ABCs anyway—just to make sure he'll score high on tests?

One way out of the trap is to realize that the charts and tests themselves have been getting low marks from plenty of experts over the years. You'll find it easier to avoid "testing trauma" if you keep in mind that the results of a test—whether it's a growth chart in the back of a child-care manual, or a readiness test administered by a private preschool—are only as reliable as the test itself. Let's take the developmental-milestone charts, for example. First of all, have you wondered why there's so much variation from one chart to the next that your baby may score like an Olympic champion on one and barely manage to keep pace with his peers in Pampers on another? One reason is that the definitions of the milestones are often fuzzy. What's "sitting," for example? A twenty-eight-week-old baby may sit with support by leaning forward on his hands for a few moments, but it's not until forty weeks that he's likely to sit steadily without using his hands for support. Furthermore, the ages referred to are based on the assumption that the pregnancy was full-term. If your baby was premature, it's important to correct for the number of weeks he came early.

As for *reading-readiness* tests, many educators and early-childhood experts are quick to criticize them. "A readiness test is an assessment of a content of knowledge that is deemed by those authors and that publisher to represent the content that a child needs in order to begin to read," says Dr. Abbott-Shim. Obviously, that means it has limitations. Dr. Edward Chittendon, a research psychologist at Educational Testing Service, states, "The content of the standardized, pencil-and-paper tests that schools give in kindergarten and first grade tends to accentuate knowledge of letters and sounds, and gives a distorted picture of what children need to know to learn to read." He points out that a reader needs to understand the concept of *story line* in order to make sense of what he is reading—the idea that a story has a beginning, middle, and end, and that a conflict will be followed by a resolution. This is learned through read-aloud and storytelling sessions. "Many children, when they come to kindergarten, can even stop to construct a story if you ask them," Dr. Chittendon says. "That ability can't be gauged by a paper-and-pencil test that asks about their letter knowledge. My criticism of the tests is that, because of their content and their format, they only assess one aspect of the knowledge that children need in order to learn to read, and that leads parents and teachers into some basic misconceptions about reading. The teacher's energy should go into doing more reading to the children, and into providing stronger literature in the school program. It shouldn't be going into flashcards."

Healthy Ways to Help

What kind of approach to testing *does* make sense? Ultimately, keep in mind that as your child's number-one fan, it's up to you to evaluate the score, based on your own understanding of him and conversations with his teacher, and to make sure the test results are used in the way that will be of most benefit to him. When you learn that your child is scheduled for testing, you'll be in a better position to evaluate the results if you ask the following questions:

- *What kind* of test is being given? Is it a screening, a developmental evaluation, or a readiness test? Has it been designed for the specific age range of the children being tested? Is the experience likely to be pleasant for most children? A screening should take no more than fifteen to twenty minutes and be fun, easy to understand, and interesting enough to elicit a child's best performance.

- *Who* will give the test? Some tests are designed to be administered by either assistants, teachers, or psychologists. However, since the authors of the major tests emphasize the importance of a child's emotional stability, attention span, muscle tone and control, perceptual abilities such as vision and hearing, fatigue, and general health status, there's really no substitute for a trained, experienced professional. In fact, according to Dr. Abbott-Shim, "Anybody trained in the field can look at the child and make as good a hunch as that Denver [screening test] will give." More important, a competent tester can offer a great deal more insight into your child's makeup than a mere test score. "With a good assessment, the feedback that I get from the tester—the psychologist who's actually administering the test—is more valuable than what the actual score says," says Dr. Abbott-Shim. "With a young child, the observations that the tester makes of the child's approach strategies and ability to analyze situations and come up with alternatives, and whether he or she continues to try and solve a problem or becomes frustrated quickly—all of those kinds of feedback are as valuable as what the actual test is getting at."

And just in case you think *you're* the best candidate for the job of tester, it would be wise to remember Dr. Abbott-Shim's earlier remark: "We need to support, encourage, and facilitate our children's development—we don't need to evaluate them."

■ Will the test be *individually* administered, or given to a *group?* Most early-childhood experts believe only an individual test is reliable at this age.

■ *Is there a parent questionnaire?* Because you live with your child day in and day out, you're probably in the best position to provide essential information about him. It can be very helpful for the school to know something about the child's developmental history and your own concerns *before* the test so that the examiner can pay special attention to potential problems. You may be asked questions about when he got his first tooth, or the age at which he began using the toilet— reflecting recent research linking physical, emotional, and cognitive development.

■ *How are the scores reported?* What do they mean? The score might be expressed simply in terms of your child being "at risk" or "not at risk" of learning problems in areas pertaining to the test. Or you may receive a *percentile* score, placing your child's performance in the context of those of other children the same age taking the test. The Denver Developmental Screening Test, for example, tells you at which age 25, 50, 75, or 90 percent of children can engage in each behavior tested. You receive a record sheet detailing how your child performed on each item, and by making comparisons you can note any developmental lag or sign of possible learning difficulties. Still other tests use a *sentence report* offering generalizations about your child's abilities based on his test performance. You might learn, for instance, that he is "generally competent in listening to a story and understanding it."

■ *How reliable is the score?* Tests of children under two are notoriously unreliable as predictors of future intelligence or school performance. Keep in mind that some tests—most notably, the Gesell—have been criticized because the "norms" are based on the performances of white, middle-class children. What you may be learning when you get the score is how your child compares with a group of white, Anglo-Saxon children from educated families. Furthermore, no matter how precise a score appears to be, each test has what is known as an "error of measurement," or range within which the score is correct plus or minus a given number of points. "It's important for parents to know that a specific test score is not the be-all and end-all of what that child would score another time, nor does it mean the child is in actuality at that level," emphasizes Dr. Abbott-Shim. "Because tests are not absolutely reliable and absolutely valid, it's important that we not interpret the test score as the specific level of a child's competence or performance."

In the long run, a test is a very limited way of evaluating a child. Obviously, living with your child day in and day out gives you a matchless opportunity to get to know what subjects and materials are most likely to catch his interest, how he goes about tackling a problem, and how his talents and inclinations resemble and differ from those of his friends. "Intelligence isn't something that you find out just by giving the child a test," says Dr. Louise Bates Ames, cofounder and associate director of the Gesell Institute and the author of numerous books on child development. "You *know* if you've got a bright child. A bright child asks interesting questions, he's interested when you read to him, he's knowledgeable, he catches onto things." A nursery-school teacher can also be of enormous help in pointing out your child's inclinations and noting potential problem areas.

If the test is intended to help you decide whether your child is ready for kindergarten, consider the results in conjunction with his nursery-school teacher's comments and your own observations. And keep in mind that a child who seems to be lagging behind the norms may in fact be highly intelligent. According to Dr. Ames, "we do see children who are what we call superior-immature. This means he was a bright baby, and he is a bright little kid. You *know* he's bright, but he is young for his age." In the long run, the most important thing to remember is that tests are valuable only insofar as they aid you in understanding your child's unique abilities and in making educational choices that will help him develop to his fullest potential.

Why Johnny
Can't Read
While Sucking
His Pacifier

Two years of age is the best time to begin if you want to expend the least amount of time and energy in teaching your child to read. (Should you be willing to go to a little trouble you can begin at eighteen months, or if you are very clever, as early as ten months of age.)
　　　—Glenn Doman, *How to Teach Your Baby to Read*

Three-Year-Olds CAN READ AND WRITE
For only $1.50 a week you can help give your child the head start needed to ensure success in school! Don't wait 5 years—begin your child's education NOW with our learning kits. Each kit provides TWO MONTHS' detailed instructional lessons in reading, writing, math, science, social studies, and arts and crafts.
　　　—*Classified advertisement in national magazine, $12 plus*
　　　$1.75 postage and handling

"Michael came home crying one day because he said he was the only one in his nursery school class who doesn't know how to write his name.

—*Mother of a four-year-old*

WELL, WHAT are you waiting for?

Do you want your child to be the only illiterate left in the neighborhood sandbox?

Now, this is a problem our grandparents never had to worry about. Early reading was frowned on during the first half of this century. The American philosopher and progressive educator John Dewey did not advocate teaching reading before first grade. And the landmark Morphett-Washburn report of 1931, which presented findings indicating that children could not and should not learn to read until they had reached a mental age of six and one-half, was a major impetus behind postponement of formal reading instruction until the first grade. But the public began to have second thoughts in 1955, with the publication of Rudolph Flesch's bestselling *Why Johnny Can't Read.* This book trumpeted the virtues of the phonetics approach to reading, claiming it was teaching British children to read years earlier than their American counterparts and hailing it as the solution to all our problems. The trend continued as the 1960s saw a revival of the Montessori movement in this country; and during the same period the introduction of educational TV shows such as "Sesame Street" had three-year-olds from coast to coast spouting their numbers and ABCs.

Today early-reading instruction is *de rigueur* for the well-rounded superbaby. In fact, no less than the Encyclopaedia Britannica Home Library is marketing Glenn Doman's Better Baby Reading Program by direct mail. For $39.95 you get a kit containing flashcards and instructions on how to start your child reading at *six months* of age, based on the course offered at Doman's Institutes for the Achievement of Human Potential in Philadelphia, and originally devised for brain-damaged children.

You start by holding up a flashcard—printed, say, with *mommy* or *daddy* in red type—and at the same time you tell baby what it says. On day two, you repeat this procedure. On the third day comes the big moment: you ask the child what the card says. The child who gives the correct answer (the "better baby," presumably) gets high praise and hugs. Pity the unfortunate infant or toddler who gets it wrong—she forfeits such affection, of course. Soon baby will learn to spout the right response, and before long, the original cards in the kit will be no more of a novelty for her than yesterday's newspaper. Then Mommy and Daddy can draw up new ones and even teach her to read a book of sorts.

Aside from the $39.95, what have you got to lose? "We know that customers are going to get varying degrees of success with the product," admits Larry Heskett, director of mail-order marketing for the Encyclopaedia Britannica Home Library Service, "but we see nothing wrong with something that's going to make the parent and child spend a lot of time together in something that's going to have a beneficial effect on the child's future. There were a number of our people here who felt it was something we could offer without being ashamed of it."

Does Britannica hope to create new generations of geniuses whose idea of a good time will be leafing through the encyclopedias? Apparently not. "The one area yet to be proven," Heskett acknowledges, "is whether these superbabies are going to be super adults."

According to many child psychologists, however, there is *much* more about the Doman program—and other methods of early-reading instruction—that is yet to be proven. Unfortunately, although there has long been evidence suggesting that the traditional first-grade introduction of reading in American schools should not have been engraved in stone, the current mad dash toward early literacy is not only unjustified on the basis of research findings but downright harmful to many kids. As Dr. Edward Zigler, Sterling professor of child psychology at Yale University and former director of the U.S. Office of Child Development, points out, Doman "likens the child to a computer that can be programmed, and the human brain to a vessel that can be filled with knowledge." By contrast, developmental psychologists such as Piaget and Gesell, says Dr. Zigler, have found the process of human learning to be far more complex and active: "Learning is seen as a naturally unfolding, sequential developmental process in the child, and the parent or teacher's role is more to nurture or foster each stage of development rather than to program or inscribe knowledge on the passive child."

Doman maintains that by showing your child flashcards, you can improve her vision and speed the development of what he calls "visual pathways" to her brain, enabling her to learn to read words at the fastest possible rate. According to Dr. Zigler, however, by eight months of age infants' vision is nearly equal to that of adults, and you can't improve their eyesight by showing them flashcards. Moreover, research shows that the development of babies' sight and hearing is directly related to *conceptional* age (the age from conception), not to time elapsed since birth; thus it's evidently developmental maturity that counts here, not environmental stimulation, because a baby's vision seems to develop at a fixed rate whether she is *in utero* or out. "An eight-month-old infant who was three months premature will have the vision of a full-term five-month-old conceived on the same date," observes Dr. Zigler, "despite the additional stimulation he has received by being in the world an extra three months."

Pointing out that Doman has failed to supply data from controlled studies with normal children to indicate that his methods work, or that Doman "graduates" grow up to be smarter, more successful, or better readers, Dr. Zigler warns that "most of the research to date in early intervention has been concerned with the child who *does not have an ordinary environment* or who is identified as being *at risk of developmental difficulties* [emphasis added]."

In fact, a normal child is undoubtedly better off with a *wide variety* of stimuli rather than a rigorous program of formal instruction. Early-childhood specialists believe that cognitive growth is achieved in many ways other than rigorous intellectual training. When your child shows natural curiosity about her new world—mouthing, sucking, biting, and manipulating objects, for example, or banging and shaking them to see whether they make noise—and you respond by letting her play with a variety of toys and household objects, you're offering much *more* than you could with a flashcard. "If handed cardboard flashcards with bright red letters . . . an infant's first instinct would be to pick them up, feel them, bang them on the floor, and put them in his mouth," notes Dr. Zigler drily.

Many child-development experts also theorize that through a child's early attachment to her parents, she learns emotional lessons that actually contribute to her cognitive growth. For example, says Dr. Zigler, by learning to influence others through her own behavior, she not only acquires a sense of security but also learns to shape and control information.

What Is Reading, Anyway?

No, don't skip to the next section. The answer to this question may *seem* obvious—it's just what you're doing at this very moment—but the process of reading is far more complex than just being able to figure out what the words on a page say. In fact, learning to read is typical of cognitive growth in general in that it requires a much wider and more complex range of skills and knowledge than a child could ever acquire through specific exercises or flashcards. To understand what reading really is, let's take a look at this classified advertisement, which appeared recently in the real-estate section of a prominent metropolitan newspaper:

29 MINUTES FROM NYC.
$329,500   COLONIAL.
Compact, mint cond, 7 rms incl 3
bdrms, 1½ newish bths, walk to
schools, quiet st, ideal starter home

If you were looking for a house, you would probably be able to decipher this ad easily. You would know, for example, that *colonial* usually does not refer to a dwelling built in 1760 but instead a style of house design with the bedrooms upstairs (as opposed to a "ranch" or "split-level"). You would also be familiar with real-estate shorthand: *mint cond* means "mint condition"; *rms* means "rooms"; *bths,* "bathrooms"; and *st,* "street." This aspect of reading is called *decoding.* There's no denying it's an essential part of the process.

But (as every househunter knows) it's only half the story. Based on the above description of this house, you might consider it ideal for your family of five or six, assuming the kids share bedrooms. Why, they can even walk to school! Reading between the lines, however, any real-estate agent would tell you that the ad contains two dead giveaways that this is not exactly South Fork (despite the price): *compact,* and *ideal starter home.* This skill is the second important component of reading: *comprehension.*

How does a househunter learn that *compact* means "small" and not, say, that there are cleverly designed storage units in every room? Or that *ideal starter home* means "tiny"—and not that there's plenty of room in the kitchen for his young family, including infant paraphernalia, three-year-old's trike, and kindergartner's guppy tank? He learns this from *experience.* Chances are he has been fooled before. These days when he reads an ad for a house that's in the right price range and seems to have all the amenities he needs, he instantly asks himself, What's wrong with it?

Without such comprehension or ability to understand what you're reading, the ability to decode is virtually useless. (If you doubt this, think back to the last time you tried to read the instructions for setting a digital watch.) For this reason, no child can become a good reader without a wealth of life experience to back her up. She needs to learn to evaluate what she is reading, and to draw conclusions. Having the confidence to do this requires self-esteem born of healthy human relationships with those who love her—not daily exposure to testing situations and so-called games designed to produce prodigies. And it also requires previous exposure to a variety of situations, materials, places, people, and emotions.

Are Early Readers Better Readers?

Suppose more children were introduced to the great storehouse of knowledge accumulated by man four or five years earlier then (*sic*) they are now? Imagine the result if Einstein could have had five extra years of creative life.
—Glenn Doman, *How to Teach Your Baby to Read*

According to this school of thought, we ought to be able to raise smarter kids by preventing them from napping and keeping them up till ten every night—thereby providing several more creative hours a day to explore "the great storehouse of knowledge accumulated by man." So far there are no controlled studies to support this theory, and as for Einstein, we'll never know.

In fact, in examining the few studies of early readers that do exist, it quickly becomes clear that rote methods such as Doman's are *not* the key. A famous 1966 study of seventy-nine early readers, done by Dolores Durkin of Columbia University, found that they shared four important experiences:

1. They were read to on a regular basis.

2. Their parents loved to read, and their homes were filled with reading matter, from books and magazines to newspapers and comics. Also, the parents took the opportunity to point out examples of useful print in the environment, from billboards and street signs to package labels and the sides of trucks.

3. Writing materials were readily available to the children. "Almost without exception," wrote Durkin, "the starting point of curiosity about written language was an interest in

scribbling and drawing. From this developed an interest in copying objects and letters of the alphabet."

4. The adults in the children's homes stimulated their interest in reading and writing by answering endless questions, praising their efforts at learning to read and write, visiting the library with them, buying books, and displaying their paperwork in a prominent place in the home (such as the refrigerator door).

Durkin's study depicted a process of learning *initiated by the child in an environment conducive to literacy,* with appropriate encouragement from responsive parents. This does not imply, however, that parents or teachers can systematically set out to produce early readers. A 1987 study of spontaneous early readers by Sarah Sparrow, chief psychologist at the Yale Child Study Center and a professor at the Yale University School of Medicine, found that most of the subject's parents *had no idea* how their children learned to read, except that they were regular viewers of "Sesame Street." "In fact, some parents of the control kids [the group that did *not* read unusually early] *had* tried to teach them how to read," notes Dr. Sparrow. Sparrow did not find early readers to be necessarily brighter, either. "They're probably not more intelligent—we have kids with IQs of one hundred who are early spontaneous readers. However, more kids in the very small group in the 150 to 160 IQ range did learn to read early." But learning to read early is far from desirable for all children, says Sparrow. "I think there are more important things for three- and four-year-olds to be doing."

As a matter of fact, there is considerable evidence to show that children who receive early *formal* reading instruction may turn out to be less avid readers in the long run. The classic studies by the educator Carleton Washburn are still frequently cited as evidence of this. Washburn studied children in the public schools of Winnetka, Illinois, comparing classes of children who were taught to read in first grade with classes who were taught in second grade. Initially the first-grade readers performed better on reading tests, but by fourth grade the others had caught up. As for the long-term results, a follow-up study made when the two groups were attending junior high school found that the children who had been taught to read later were more enthusiastic about reading than their counterparts in the early group.

Or consider three studies done in the early 1980s by researchers at the University of Haifa, in Israel. Twelve members of a kibbutz kindergarten class, whose ages ranged from five to seven years of age, were taught to decode. Within four calendar months the six oldest children in the group had all acquired the rudiments of decoding; but of the six youngest children, only one had done so. In a second study, the five oldest and five youngest children in three different kindergartens were instructed by well-trained first-grade teachers under controlled conditions. Again, the older group did significantly better. In a third study the same researchers found that among first-graders older children outperformed younger ones in reading comprehension.

"Proving that some young children can indeed be taught to read well before school-entry age and may even derive benefit from this skill does not necessarily mean that the majority of children should receive formal reading instruction in their preschool years," the researchers concluded. "The great amount of time young children spend nowadays in educational settings could perhaps be put to better use by promoting language competence and high-level cognitive skills and affective coping mechanisms, rather than by direct teaching of school-related skills." Note the researchers' choice of words: they advocate *promoting* various skills—not drilling or training.

Reading Readiness

For many parents, the phrase *reading readiness* seems to conjure up an image of a child poised on a diving board, prepared to plunge suddenly into the pool of literacy. Reading specialists term this the "know-nothing" approach to reading readiness: you assume that until your child knows his ABCs and the fact that each letter on a page represents a sound, he hasn't learned anything at all about reading.

Fortunately, there's a lot more to reading readiness than that. According to researcher Catherine E. Snow of Harvard, writing in the *Harvard Educational Review,* the most important contribution parents make to their children's reading readiness is to prepare them to understand and produce something called *decontextualized language,* or the kind of speech used in stories, in which the author or narrator is impersonal, the setting is unfamiliar, and the language and sentence structure are relatively complex. For example, when my son hears me read, "Late one summer afternoon Lisa and her mother took their laundry to the laundromat," at the beginning of *A Pocket for Corduroy,* he is willing to listen even though (a) he doesn't know anyone named Lisa, and (b) he's never been to a laundromat. Having heard many books over the past three and one-half years, he knows that if he's patient and attentive chances are that in this one he'll meet an interesting character or two and hear a good story.

Contrary to popular belief, says Snow, children of *all* socioeconomic levels encounter print as part of their daily life. But it is through repeated experience with words in a variety of contexts (as opposed to those in a single context, such as, say, the words *Burger King* on a box of fries, or the sign on a storefront) that children from educated, middle-class families arrive at school with an advantage over their less privileged counterparts. "Children need both literacy and decontextualized language skills to succeed at school," writes Snow. "But it may be that literacy skills are simple enough to be acquired at school, whereas developing the skill of using language in a decontextualized way relies more heavily on experiences *only home can provide* [emphasis added]."

What a relief! Personally, I'd much rather read my kids books about outer space, insects, and French mice who play the piano than suffer through spelling drills. And looking at the development of reading readiness as a gradual process that takes place over a period of years, it's amazing to realize how much a child can learn about reading *every day,* without a single flashcard. Through the preschool years you are preparing your child to read by helping her learn

- To understand and follow directions

- To recognize similarities and differences (Can she tell the difference between a robin and a bluejay? One day she'll notice how a *b* differs from a *d.*)

- To understand spatial concepts, such as more, less, near, and far

- Word meanings

- How words rhyme

- To recognize and interpret pictures ("Why is the man standing on the corner? What is he waiting for? Where is he going?")

- That some words begin with the same sound while others begin with different sounds

- To remember the main points of a story and to retell them

- How to evaluate facts and draw conclusions ("Why did the little pig go to the fair half an hour earlier than he told the wolf?")

- To predict the outcome of a story

- To name and recognize the letters of the alphabet and numerals

Signs of Reading Readiness

Before you start setting up the blackboard in the playroom, keep in mind that children pass through many "prereading stages" before they are really ready to read. Although your child may show one or more signs of passage, it's important to wait until she goes through a considerable number of these stages before you begin to think about introducing her to reading at home.

A child who knows the alphabet, can make up rhymes, and understands the relationship between sounds and letters may be ready to read. Taking the initiative, however, and drilling these skills into a child who as yet shows little inclination will not necessarily *cause* reading readiness—any more than putting on a leotard guarantees to turn you or me into Jane Fonda.

Besides, some of the skills found in most so-called readiness programs—such as learning to sound out words phonetically, identifying rhymes, and completing shapes—are difficult for some preschoolers to master at any stage. As educator Bonnie Lass points out, maybe that says more about the programs than the kids: "These skills are unnecessary for acquiring a rather large sight vocabulary and zest for books. It seems important to differentiate . . . between skills necessary for reading and those required for success in formal reading programs."

A child who is ready to read

1. Has developed a wide spoken vocabulary

2. Knows most of the letters of the alphabet and understands that they represent spoken sounds

3. Can make up rhymes

4. Shows an interest in being read to

5. Insists that you or she hold the book right side up

6. Turns pages one at a time

7. Points to words in a story she knows well

8. Can identify some road signs and product names on packages

9. Understands that you can recognize words not only by their context, but by the letters that make them up (as one expert put it, knows "that *bun* is not *bug*")

10. Asks to be taught to read

All Children Are Early Readers

EARLY READING CAN BE FUN-TASTIC!

Why wait? If your preschooler is ready—and he or she probably is—you can teach your child to read *now,* and provide a headstart on learning that spells success for the future.
—*Cover blurb,* Barbara J. Fox, *Teach Your Child To Read in 20 Minutes a Day,* 1986

Put your wallet back in your pocket. The good news is that without any fancy programs or "learning kits," your child has been developing the skills she will need in order to learn to read ever since the day she was born. Every story you read aloud, every crayon scribble on the wallpaper represents a stage in the process of learning to read which has come to be called "emergent literacy."

Unfortunately, as Judith A. Schickendanz points out in *More than the ABCs: The Early Stages of Reading and Writing* (1986), we tend to underestimate the importance of these early efforts. "Ask parents when their child started to talk, and they will give the age at which the child *began* to use some well-articulated words, not the age when the child began to utter well-formed grammatical sentences," she says. "But ask parents or teachers when a child began to read or to write, and they are reluctant to give the child credit until behavior matches the conventional, or adult, model. Scribbling and retelling familiar story books tend to be discounted as merely pretend, not real, writing and reading."

In her often-quoted article, "Portrait of My Son as an Early Reader," published in *The Reading Teacher* in October 1982, Bonnie Lass, an education instructor at Boston College, gives an account of her son Jed's reading-related behavior, which started in infancy. "At two weeks he stared raptly at the letters on our T-shirts," she notes and goes on to describe how, provided with plenty of hand-me-down books to touch, taste, and otherwise explore, Jed showed a strong interest in books as playthings. He also enjoyed read-aloud sessions with his parents, learning to turn the page during storytime and delighting in the stories themselves. Then he learned Mother Goose rhymes and, walking along a busy street, would yell out the names and numbers of all the stores. With encouragement from his parents, Jed learned to recognize his own name ("We printed his name on fogged-up car windows and shower doors"), then words in context and finally out of context.

Long before they learn to decode, children who have regular contact with books develop an understanding of how books "work." Watch your child as she sits with *Pat the Bunny* or her favorite chewable vinyl volume. Before she is a year old, she already understands that a book has pages that can be turned. As she begins to pretend to read, she will probably start out inventing sentences that sound like her own speech. Soon, however, she will begin to talk "like a book."

When my three-year-old son recently decided to "read" a book to his seven-month-old sister, he opened to a picture of a cow and began, "Once upon a time there was a cow, and he wanted to get married." Turning the page, he continued: "So he asked his mommy if it was okay, and then he got married and lived happily ever after." Confused though he may be about bovine sexuality, my son clearly has grasped two important concepts about books: he understands that the style of literary language is different from that of speech (using such phrases as "once upon a time," and "happily ever after"), and he knows that a story has a beginning, middle, and end. As he learns to read, having internalized this framework will help him feel confident and comfortable with books. Perhaps most important, he believes that reading to his sister is a great way to entertain her, a sure sign that he has already developed a positive attitude about books that will keep him motivated when the time comes to learn to decode.

Another fundamental concept, which reading teachers call *print awareness,* is also developing during the preschool years. Around the house and outdoors, children see print, and they see the people around them using this print for various meaningful purposes—writing a shopping list, leaving a note for the baby-sitter, labeling a jacket for nursery school. You can encourage your child's print awareness by providing plenty of writing tools (crayons, markers, pencils, magic slate) so that she can "write" whenever she feels the urge. And in the course of your day, point out how you use print as a tool to obtain necessary information—from newspapers, food-packaging labels, cookbooks, and maps. What you're doing is setting an example—and when the time comes, your child will want to read and write just like Mom and Dad.

As your child learns, it's important not to expect the road to literacy to lead forever onward and upward. In fact, reading and writing are likely to be—as with virtually everything else about raising kids—a matter of going two steps forward and one step back. As researchers at the University of Kentucky point out in their 1981 study of print awareness in preschoolers, "Children do not discard earlier forms of writing altogether when they become capable of creating more mature forms." A four-and-a-half-year-old girl who knew how to write her own name as well as *MOM* and *DAD,* for instance, would resort to scribbling when she wanted to produce a lot of writing. Preschoolers who are becoming interested in writing often invent spellings and even letters. But not to worry. Making it clear to your child that you appreciate *any* form of written expression, rather than correcting her attempts to write letters or her spelling, will encourage her efforts and bring out her best in the long run.

Kids Will Be Kids

> Janet Gauger and Neal Gauger (8 months). Neal has been on The Early Development Program since birth. He now reads over 2,000 words and sentences, and recognizes over two thousand Bits of Intelligence. His home program includes math, swimming, music, Japanese, and French.
> —*Photo caption,* Glenn Doman's *How to Multiply Your Baby's Intelligence*

No matter how bright your child, no matter how eager she may be to get through *Where the Wild Things Are* all by herself, let's face it: reading-readiness activities don't occur in a vacuum, and the normal emotional development of a toddler or preschooler often tends to interfere with book learning. After all, you have to sit down—or at least stand still—in order to read the words on a page. Sitting is not something little kids spend much time doing. They're smart enough to know there's a whole world out there filled with new sights, sounds, tastes, smells, and people just waiting to be explored.

And the emotional dynamics of the parent-child relationship, as well as of your child's developmental stage of the moment, are forever intruding on the reading lesson. When my son Matthew was in the throes of being a two-year-old, for example, I sent for the Better Baby Reading Program and tried displaying Glenn Doman's *mommy* card to him. True to form, he quickly grabbed it from my hand. *"I* have it," he declared. *"You* can't have it.

I'm reading it." We sent back the flashcards before the ten-day guarantee elapsed, but we're still working on learning to share and take turns—lessons that do not promise to earn him the Nobel Prize for literature but will, I hope, at least keep him out of jail.

Bonnie Lass describes a similar episode with her child in "Portrait of My Son as an Early Reader." Jed actually began to decode before the age of three, and Mom would help him over the rough spots. "In response to . . . miscues, I would simply supply the right word," writes Lass. "Jed usually accepted it, but in the case of 'hound' for *Honda,* we had a tug-of-words. Each of us insisted on our reading of the word until his tears brought me to my senses. A two-year-old who is beginning to read is still a two-year-old. And, I suppose, if a Rabbit is a car, why not a dog?" Just as the most agile one-year-old may be unable to reach the pedals on a trike simply because her legs are too short, even the most book-hungry preschooler's literacy can only develop within the context—and constraints—of her emotional development. As her relationship with you develops, as she copes with issues such as separation, and as her self-esteem grows, the profound changes she is experiencing will be reflected in every aspect of her behavior, from toileting to tantrums to reading-readiness activities.

Lass gives another example of this, noting that at times Jed would ask his parents to read words for him with which he had long been familiar, apparently reluctant to read without Mommy and Daddy's help. "It seems certain," Lass writes, "that one cannot divorce the issue of independent reading from the larger notion of self-reliance."

Nor should we try. Why worry because your child would rather show you her latest bowel movement waiting to be flushed than her ability to parrot so-called Bits of Intelligence? According to most experts in early child development, her self-esteem and secure attachment to you are the foundation for a lifelong love of reading and learning.

Read Me a Book, Mom

"The first thing Sam does in the morning is go outside and bring in the newspaper from the driveway so we can read the baseball scores together. He can already pick out the names of some of the teams—the Pirates, the Braves, and the Mets—and read the scores."

—Father of a four-year-old boy

Reading aloud—whether it's *Charlotte's Web* or the sports section—has been shown in study after study to be the single biggest predictor of reading success in school. During regular read-aloud sessions with their parents, children grow to understand a great deal about what they can learn from books and how. Perhaps most important, they learn to associate books with warm feelings—sitting in Mom or Dad's lap and spending some special time alone together, laughing, learning, feeling close.

A woman whose three-year-old was receiving formal reading instruction grumbled to me, "He's been reading nothing but *pat, cat, hat,* and *bat* for ages. We're both bored to death!" Why make him suffer through hours of phonetics drills and ABC memorization when instead you could be opening his eyes to all the wonderful things he can learn from books read aloud? And the more you read and talk about together, the more you'll be able to read and know your child understands, because each book brings new people, places, and ideas into his world.

Woodrow Wilson, generally considered one of our more intellectual Presidents, did not learn his ABCs until he was nine, and could not read until he was eleven, according to the authors of *Cradles of Eminence.* Instead, his father read to him. "He could not wait for Woodrow to learn to read the books he himself enjoyed and wanted his son to enjoy," they write. "The brilliant and verbal minister kept the boy home, read to him, explained the meaning of what he read, then asked for Woodrow's reaction to the ideas of the book."

Few of us would choose to go to that extreme. But recent studies of the different approaches parents take in reading aloud to their children do corroborate one aspect of the elder Wilson's methods. According to one study, children whose parents *initiate talks* with them about the books they are reading seem to be better readers. Researchers theorize that this is a way of preparing a child for classroom discussion. You're helping her develop her oral language ability, as she learns to answer questions and discuss her experiences and impressions coherently. During your read-aloud sessions, you can help increase your child's print awareness in a variety of ways—as it comes naturally, and only when your child seems genuinely interested:

- Ask questions before you begin ("Is this the one where Curious George goes to jail?").

- Ask *informational* questions ("Why does the drum on a cement mixer turn?").

- Ask *anticipatory* questions ("So *then* what did the Runaway Bunny say he would do?").

- Ask *evaluative* questions ("Why did Wilbur feel scared?").

- Ask *follow-up* questions ("Would *you* like to make your own summer snowman?" "Do you remember when we went to the zoo and saw the pandas?") that connect what you've read to your child's everyday life.

- Do what reading specialists call "oral cloze exercises," a highfalutin term for the simple game in which you leave out a word in a sentence for your child to fill in ("and the dish ran away with the ———?").

- Suggest that your child choose a book and "read" it to you. When she reaches a more advanced level of understanding of the reading process, she may refuse, realizing that she doesn't really know how to read. Try dragging out some wordless picture books from her babyhood.

- Ask your child to retell a story that you recently read aloud. Write down the retelling and turn it into a book, which you can read aloud. You might even want to ask your child to draw illustrations for her favorite parts.

- During the story, when you're feeling frustrated about your preschooler's "interruptions," keep in mind that according to the same study, the children with the highest proficiency in reading were those who talked more about the story and asked more questions during the reading process. When you're tempted to tell her to be quiet and listen, remember that she's showing interest and trying her best to make sense of the story in her own mind.

During storytime children increase their print awareness, learning a great deal about the *form* of books as well as the contents. Gradually, they come to understand the relationship between print and speech, and that words are composed of groups of letters. As educator Frank Smith explains in *Insult to Intelligence* (1986), "Their greatest insight about written language before they come to school is probably that written language is different from the pattern on the wallpaper—that signs and labels have a purpose, that they *do* something more than just decorate the landscape." Unlike kids in formal early-reading programs, your child can learn these ideas without pressure and in the context of a loving, enjoyable exchange with you—as long as you resist the temptation to turn storytime into a lesson. The key is to keep it relaxed and informal, and not overdo it. Some more nonstressful ways to increase print awareness:

- Show your child the title of each book as you read it. From time to time, point out familiar letters ("Look! Do you see what letter *Velveteen* begins with?").

■ Toddlers love to turn the page. With new books, tell her when to turn; with well-thumbed volumes, make a game out of having her guess the right time to turn.

■ Move a finger along under the print to help demonstrate that we read from left to right, and from top to bottom.

■ Read books with repeated words or phrases.

■ Introduce new books often to maintain excitement, but don't neglect old favorites. The more a child sees the same set of words, the more familiar they will become.

■ Give clear answers to her questions about letter names and words, and provide illustrations. According to Snow's Harvard study, this kind of responsiveness on the part of adults to a child's demonstration of interest continues and develops that interest.

Although these techniques can help your child understand the reading process, keep in mind that your *most* important job in reading aloud is to make it a joyful, loving experience that will give her a lifelong love of books. (For this reason, most child-development experts also recommend that tape-recorded books—no matter how useful as a means of helping the child associate the written word with spoken sound—be used only as a supplement to the old-fashioned flesh-and-blood storytime.) Don't force-feed reading readiness to your child. Try only the techniques that seem to be appropriate responses to what she's really interested in.

The Right Book at the Right Age

According to *Publishers Weekly,* today's parents are reading to their children at increasingly younger ages. Although publishers once shied away from suggesting that babies as young as five months might enjoy board books, today there are entire series published for infants, starting at two months. One publisher explained rather hopefully, "The books help their eyes to focus."

Some, though not all, young babies do enjoy books, but this depends both on the parents' approach and the baby's personality. According to a 1986 report, when researchers at the University of Florida videotaped thirteen mothers reading to their infants as young as three and one-half months old, they found varying rates of success. "What made the difference," the report concludes, "was the degree to which the mothers adjusted their book-reading behavior to the developmental levels of their infants."

For starters, don't expect your infant to sit still for all of *Treasure Island;* the Florida researchers estimated the average length of an effective read-aloud session with an infant at *three minutes.* If your baby becomes distracted or seems to lose interest, don't push her, say the researchers, or storytime will end in tears. Of course, you can bring out books at different times of the day, accumulating as much as half an hour of reading altogether. But try to make it a part of your routine you'll both anticipate—at naptime, bedtime, or any regular time when your child is willing and you have a few minutes.

Keep in mind that your baby's emotional and neurological development, as well as her personality, will have enormous impact on her "love of literature." At three months, my son stared intently at each page of his first board book (a collection of pictures of vehicles, the first of many). But at that age my daughter was just getting over her colic, and we were grateful for a few moments of silence, let alone storytime. By age two, she loved books. What it all boils down to, as the Florida researchers put it, is "either infants are content to sit and listen or they are not."

When your baby *is* content to sit and listen, you should enjoy books together in an unpressured, age-appropriate way. Here are some suggestions:

Birth to Three Months: It's not easy to hold a baby and a book at the same time. Board books and zigzag (accordion-style) books, which stand up by themselves, solve that problem. Your newborn will enjoy nursery rhymes, songs you remember from your own childhood, or anything you like to sing. (Our infants were subjected to all the early Beatles, as well as our favorites from Simon and Garfunkel.) Any doggerel you can make up with baby's name included is bound to be a hit, and action songs ("Trot, trot to Boston," and so on) are fun for parent and baby. Most babies try to devour books—literally—and while you won't want her to cut her teeth on your treasured childhood copy of *Little Women,* do have a board book or cloth book for the purpose.

Four to Six Months: Now babies love to reach and grasp, and everything goes into the mouth. For this purpose, they will favor cloth and soft vinyl books, which (although they usually have tacky illustrations) are easily grasped and chewed. You will like them because they don't disintegrate after such treatment. If you insist on reading to baby despite her determination to chew, some mothers suggest offering a saliva-proof book, teething ring, or even a finger to gnaw while you turn the pages of *Pat the Bunny.* (Chances are, she won't lag dangerously behind her peers if you wait a few months, though.) If she's sitting up, give her yesterday's newspaper and watch her shred it.

Seven to Nine Months: At this point babies may be more interested in looking at the pictures, and you can begin to point and label things ("That's a doll, and that's a train . . ."). On the other hand, they're usually eager to practice crawling at this stage, and sitting around with their nose in a book may not be at the top of their list.

Nine to Twelve Months: Now your baby really can begin to enjoy the contents of a book. She'll like board books because the pages can be turned easily by chubby fingers. And she may begin to point to illustrations, smile at familiar pictures, and laugh at funny noises you make ("The piggy goes, *'Oink! oink!' "*). Clear, bright pictures of familiar objects have the most appeal. The University of Florida study found that babies of all ages looked longest at books that were colorful and familiar.

Twelve to Eighteen Months: Now that they're mobile, they can find their favorites and toddle over to you with requests, although they may not stand still long enough to hear you read them. Babies at this stage *love* repetition. When our son was around a year old, my husband and I used to find ourselves reading *Pat the Bunny* so often we'd hide it to maintain our sanity. Leave a few board books around so that they can turn the pages and pretend to read. And save old magazines; the baby will delight in pointing to pictures and asking, "What's that?" No matter what you're reading, ham it up: "Oh, look! A *dump truck!* What's it doing? Yes, dumping! Yay!"

Nineteen to Thirty Months: At last you can read real stories. Anything about their complex emotional lives will be a big hit—sibling rivalry, using the potty, sharing toys, and missing Mommy and Daddy when they go out. Your selections should also reflect your own values and your child's passions of the moment, whether they be animals, vehicles, or an upcoming holiday.

Healthy Ways to Help

Learning to read and write requires a much broader range of skills than mere letter recognition. Your child's future reading ability will be enhanced by virtually *anything* you do to expand her world and her abilities to understand it. There's no need to turn your home into boot camp; just use each occasion as it arises.

Here are some ideas, recommended by parents and educators, to help you encourage your child to develop all the skills she will need to become a competent and enthusiastic reader:

- Help her develop her powers of observation (needed to see the words on a page, but also needed to develop her knowledge of and curiosity about the world around her). Go for walks, watch the birds, compare different leaves, trees, and bugs. On city streets, watch for daily changes in shop windows, interesting people, different cars and trucks. Indoors, play "I spy": start with a simple version ("I spy with my little eye . . . an M&M on the floor!") and work up to "I spy four blue things on the table." Lotto and memory games keep them hopping, too. Give her practice in classifying objects: ask her to help sort the laundry, or empty the dishwasher's silverware basket. Puzzles are another fun way to sharpen the eye.

- Help her to develop eye-hand coordination (needed for holding a pencil and writing letters, which is one of the major ways children seem to internalize the alphabet) by providing plenty of art materials—brushes and paint, markers, pencils, crayons, modeling clay. A child under the age of two can use stacking cups, boxes with tops, pots and pans—and also books. Pegboards and tiles, as well as small household objects that can be turned into collages (pasta or paper clips), will also help. Try sewing with a blunt needle and thread, or with a toy lacing kit. Or show your child how to make a necklace by stringing small beads or Cheerios onto thread.

- Have on hand a variety of forms of print—from coupons to catalogs to labels to magnetic letters—for your child to play with and use as she needs them. An old typewriter is also a favorite feature of the junior "home office."

- Encourage pretend play. When your child puts on a fire hat and pretends to spray the furniture with a hose, ask questions, remind her of a similar scene you've recently read about, and get her talking about what she's imagining. Before you toss anything into the garbage, ask yourself whether your child might love to have it—this includes old clothes for dress-up, play money, old maps, containers from the kitchen, grocery store circulars, envelopes, junk mail, and other props that will inspire her. What does pretend play have to do with reading? Many developmental specialists believe it helps a child feel comfortable with the idea of symbols—that one thing can stand for another, whether it's a block for a boat or the letters *D-O-G* for the family pet.

■ Give her plenty of opportunity and space for running, jumping, and other forms of exercise. This will aid her general development, expand her vocabulary (bringing such prepositions as *over* and *under* to life), and enhance her "body concept," or understanding of how her own body consists of the sum of its parts—one of the earliest forms of abstraction.

■ As your child gets older, play games like "grandmother's trunk": bring out a shoebox or old suitcase and, together, pack it with objects beginning with the same letter of the alphabet.

Do Workbooks Work?

"You know what's great? Timmy's reached the stage where he can just zip through a workbook all by himself, one page after another."

—Mother of a four-year-old

What keeps a child busy for at least twenty minutes, can be carried anywhere, and promises to deliver reading readiness, all for only $1.95? You guessed it—a preschool workbook. There's no denying the appeal of these books. After all, they don't cost much, they seem a lot more stimulating than coloring books, they're ostensibly designed for this age group, and they're written by people with all sorts of credentials (One series solemnly notes that the artist and art director have a B.A. and a B.S., respectively!). What could possibly be wrong with them?

Plenty, according to William Hooks of the Bank Street College of Education Media Group, himself a coauthor of a series of preschool workbooks. "The typical workbooks are for children younger than four, and workbooks are not even appropriate at that age," he says. "That kind of time would be better spent with a hands-on approach to sensory materials. A three-year-old is much better off playing with blocks, or any other kind of toy for that matter. A workbook is far too abstract—there are thousands of other experiences they should be having at that age."

But for parents who make sure Junior takes plenty of visits to the zoo and the firehouse, surely half an hour a day spent on reading readiness can only prove beneficial? "If you don't show them how it links back with their daily life, it's pretty meaningless," says Hooks. "A child may learn to decode, but it may turn him off to reading forever."

No matter how bright your child, the workbook format presents a number of problems, particularly for the younger preschooler. First, workbooks assume a kind of linear thinking few young children engage in—and which many developmental specialists feel runs counter to their fresh, creative way of viewing the world. When Matthew and I "worked on" an exercise in patterning, he was delighted at being able to guess the next step in a series *bat-ball-bat-ball-bat-ball.* When he came to the next set, a group of faces, *happy-sad-happy-sad-happy-sad,* he sat staring at the page. "Why is he sad?" he asked mournfully, and proceeded to speculate on all the "mean things" that had happened to the poor face. (I took comfort in the thought that he was practicing the skill known as "perspective-taking.")

Second, despite the warnings on many workbooks, parents often persist in viewing them as part of independent play—something that will keep a preschooler busy for a good fifteen minutes while Mom or Dad fixes dinner. "We think there should be some interaction at this age. Doing the activities *with* the child leads to all kinds of insights," explains Dr. Hooks. "But it's important to keep in mind that you're there to discuss and interact, not just to say whether he's got the right or wrong answer."

Finally, many educators question the usefulness of workbooks for *any* age group, on the grounds that they are a dull, uncreative approach to learning and don't really teach much, anyway. "Don't worry, they get more of these worksheets than you ever wanted once they get to elementary school," a nursery-school teacher told me in disgust. Frank Smith sums up the typical workbook exercise when he asks in *Insult to Intelligence,* "Has anyone ever met a child who could not tell the difference between a boat and a dog?"

"I Think I Bought the Wrong Mobile": The Tyranny of "Toys That Teach"

Lil Red Shovel (France): Here's the perfect little shovel for a child's little hands! Its big handle and large scoop make it perfect for moving sand, snow, or loose dirt. Educational Play Value: Coordination, gross motor skills, creative play. . . . $4.98

—Discovery Toys catalog

"Your Busy Box plays music? Gee, ours doesn't. Where'd you get it? I guess I got the wrong one."

—Mother of a nine-month-old boy

"One of the delights of my life is when parents buy one of those 'toys that teach' and the child throws it away and plays with the box."

—Edward Zigler, Sterling professor of psychology at Yale University and former director of the U.S. Office of Child Development

PERSONALLY, if I invested in one of those "toys that teach" from a fancy toy store or catalog, I'd be pretty depressed to find my kids playing with the box. In a recent Childcraft catalog, a humble pogo stick (probably good for developing gross motor skills) was listed at $28.95. Then there's the plastic teeter-totter for $44.95 (which helps teach the principles of gravity?), the collage kit for $18.95, and the toy dressing table (pink, of course) for $49.95. A generation ago parents would have worried that spending so much money on mere toys would be spoiling a child. Today's parents, on the other hand, worry that deprived of all these "educational" toys our kids will never make it through kindergarten, let alone the Ivy League.

And the advertisers know it, of course. Lately it seems as though *every* toy is an educational toy. Even electronic talking stuffed animals (at over fifty dollars apiece) are marketed as "active educational entertainment, nurturing language in the child"—thanks to the broad vocabularies of their cassette recordings and their ability to engage children in "interactive" conversation! (What makes them better than a real live adult who can not only *talk* but *listen?*) Take the Amazing Bingo Bear from Hasbro, which has a four-hundred-word vocabulary and speaks more than one hundred random phrases; likewise Cricket, a twenty-five-inch doll put out by Playmates Toys, whose mouth movement is synchronized to special encoded tapes. In advertisements for Cricket one self-styled expert makes the brilliant observation that "a toy which talks and seems to listen encourages the child's language and communication skills and teaches the child how to be a good listener." Hearing the Amazing Bingo Bear's one hundred random phrases for hours on end sounds like wonderful preparation for an acting career in Ionesco plays, or treating patients with Tourette's syndrome, but it hardly seems a good way for a child to learn to listen to typical adult human beings.

To make matters worse, not only is it vital that you have the *right* toys, but you're supposed to acquire new ones every six weeks to keep up with your child's development (and ensure her "progression" to the next stage, of course). Open virtually any manual on child development and you'll find a month-by-month list of toys designed to challenge baby's skills.

Such charts are well-intentioned, no doubt, and aimed at countering the practice of previous generations of parents who believed babies didn't do very much. Today's parents, however, are getting the message that kids require nothing less than Johnson and Johnson's Child Development Toy series, a direct-mail program for infants under *nine months* that ships out an "age-appropriate" toy (complete with a fourteen-page "activity booklet") every six weeks or so. The company runs full-page ads in major magazines explaining such subtleties as "Why we use red stripes on our rattle," noting that "every part of our rattle is there for a reason. The teething ring encourages handling skills. The blue beads provide auditory stimulation. Even the number of beads has been selected to develop tracking abilities. So even though these are playthings for your baby, they're also the most advanced learning instruments to be called toys." These "learning instruments" are cleverly marketed as "the right toys at the right time": In the magazine *Juvenile Merchandising,* Johnson and Johnson's Peter Soderberg, the toy division's director of marketing and sales, was quoted as saying that new toys are sent to mothers "at the correct intervals." Correct for whom? The assumption is that children need toys expressly designed to help them develop a given skill at a precise moment in time, the way various Nautilus machines are meant to strengthen different muscle groups. But as we have seen, this is not an assumption shared by all child psychologists. Given the realities of the marketplace, one could be forgiven for thinking this trend has more to do with sales figures than child psychology. Next we'll be hearing that Book-of-the-Month Club ships best-sellers on a schedule designed for the benefit of the developmentally normal adult!

Not everyone says you have to *buy* lots of toys, mind you. There are plenty of books that offer instructions on how to *make* age-appropriate toys for your child in your spare time. (Don't these authors realize that parents of young children are usually just as short on time as money?) Your child's IQ won't suffer a bit for lack of expensive toys as long as you give up sleep altogether and get busy assembling brain-teasers out of flour, water, spools of thread, melted wax, egg cartons, and the like.

Just in case you thought your child could enjoy simply crawling around the house, for example, the authors of *Smart Toys for Babies from Birth to Two* (1981), Kent Garland Burtt and Karen Kalkstein, point out that you have a responsibility to build a more creative crawling environment. "Crawling is more fun for a baby when he has an interesting enclosure to enter, investigate, hide in, peer out of, and leave behind in a flash of swiftly moving limbs," they observe breathlessly. To this end, they suggest building a rather elaborate "crawler's tunnel," piecing together several strong cardboard cartons with windows and doors cut out, pictures glued to the inside walls and covered with contact paper, and fabric glued all around the windows and doors. (You're made to think that something must be wrong with using a simple old, unimproved cardboard box. Or that any self-respecting infant considers crawling underneath a chair or table an utter bore.) The authors also recommend creating a peekaboo game by drawing a face on a piece of colored construction paper ("You may glue on doilies for a lace collar"), backing it with cardboard, taping a cloth over it to cover the picture, and hanging it, through two punched holes, with yarn. "Tie game to crib or playpen rail for independent investigation," they instruct. "When together with baby, hold cardboard and flip curtain up and down with appropriate exclamations, such as 'All gone!' and 'Peekaboo!' " What's wrong with covering your face—the most fascinating face in the whole world to your child—with your plain old-fashioned hands? The answer is, absolutely nothing. Unless you actually *enjoy* assembling these creations, your child will grow and develop just fine as long as he has access to simple toys (a ball, pots and pans, cardboard boxes, blocks, and the like) and caring adults and children with which to share them.

Does the Right Toy Make a Bright Boy—or Girl?

Today everybody seems to take it for granted that the right toy makes a bright boy (or girl, as the case may be). How did we all end up convinced of that? For centuries, children played with very few objects that were specifically designated as toys, aside from dolls, puppets, hoops, and balls. And according to Philippe Ariès in his classic *Centuries of Childhood* (1962), many of these were actually intended to be played with by adults as often as children. Even at the beginning of the twentieth century, most toys were simply miniature versions of adult objects—dolls with their own beauty parlors, for example.

But by the 1920s, nursery schools began to open around the country. And as researchers began for the first time to study in depth the needs and preferences of preschoolers, specially designed toys, like the ones marketed for today's under-fives, began to be introduced. Parents, however, were not immediately won over. "For some time nursery schools were almost the sole market, for the general public accepted the new, bare, primitive-looking toys rather slowly," according to Inez and Marshall McClintock's *Toys in America* (1961). "They had become so accustomed to toys that imitated adult articles that they did not readily buy these toys that looked like nothing in the grown-up world." But the commercial potential of these things was evident, and soon enough a new kind of toy business began. The Playskool Manufacturing Company was founded in 1928, Fisher-Price Toys in 1932, and Childhood Interests in 1939. "Some of the first ideas for Playskool toys came from materials used in IQ tests—the fitting of square pegs into square holes, etc.," observe the McClintocks, "which youngsters obviously enjoyed whether the toys were educational or not." Anticipating Johnson and Johnson's Child Development Toys, Childhood Interests marketed Right-Time toys under the guidance of the Gesell Clinic in New Haven, Connecticut. They were pioneers in providing playthings for babies still in their cribs, including the Cradle

Gym (later embellished with a music box) and Play-Pen-Rail Train.

Even in those days, a few malcontents groused about the trend. By 1969, journalist Ron Goulart was complaining in *The Assault on Childhood* that "Creative Playthings has been successful, and most creative, in finding new ways to sell cardboard and wood. This isn't to say that many of their toys aren't useful and valid. But they are vastly overpriced. Not to mention oversold and overpromoted. CP's copy promises miracles of education and insight, all described in a style so smug and pompous." In a *Life* magazine article, William K. Zinsser grumbled, "My quarrel with Creative Playthings is not with the playthings they create. What I resent is the language that certifies toys as edifying." Then he must have looked into his crystal ball: "Creative Playthings is leading us all into joyless new ground."

In 1986, the Toy Manufacturers of America reported a staggering $55 million in shipments in the "Preschool Learning Toys" category alone. In fact, *shipments of preschool learning toys have shot up $22 million, or a whopping 67 percent, since 1985.* With nearly 22 million preschoolers in this country, that's an increase of over one dollar's worth of toys for *every* child five and under in a single year, according to statistics compiled by the U.S. Bureau of the Census. Clearly, "leading us all into joyless new ground" is paying off for the toymakers in a big way. Why have today's supposedly sophisticated parents been so willing to follow their lead? Because we've all been marching to the beat of child-care writers and advertisers who are chanting scientific-sounding terms borrowed—and usually misapplied—from child-development theory.

At Home in the Child-Development Lab

First, identify the block in all the detail he understands. Then turn it on end and trace the quality you want him to learn. 'Triangle. A red wood block in the shape of a trian-

gle. Can you say triangle?' Now introduce the distinguishing characteristics of a triangle. Do this by placing the block horizontally on the floor (so that the triangular shape is visible on each end). 'See? A triangle has a big bottom and a point at the top. Now watch. I'll roll it over on its side, and look! It still has a big bottom and a point at the top.'
—*Give Your Child a Superior Mind,* by Siegfried and Therese Engelmann, 1966

It's hard to believe that some of us learned to recognize a triangle by simply *playing* with blocks!

How could parents ever be persuaded that they'd be doing a better job by giving lessons in the nursery—and such idiotic ones, with so little relevance to the way young children really learn, at that? As we saw in Chapter Two, the child-development pioneer Jean Piaget unwittingly encouraged the trend toward making the home a laboratory, with toys as experimental apparatus (and babies as guinea pigs, of course). After all, Piaget based much of his theory on clinical observation of the antics of his own children, so that his writings often have the flavor of an erudite baby album. Instead of recording each baby's first smile, he made careful notes of their first attempts at swiping and grasping. Consider, for example, the toy parrot that belonged to Piaget's ten-month-old daughter, Jacqueline. Once upon a time it might have functioned as a cuddly. Not in the Piaget household; there it became a tool in the study of "object permanence":

Jacqueline looks at the parrot on her lap. I place my hand on the object; she raises it and grasps the parrot. I take it away from her and, before her eyes, I move it away very slowly and put it under a rug, 40 cm. away. Meanwhile I place my hand on her lap again. As soon as Jacqueline ceases to see the parrot she looks at her lap, lifts my hand and hunts beneath it.

But Piaget's intention in hiding the toy was not to *teach* the principle of object permanence (the idea that an object still exists even when hidden from view); he was simply observing how his child naturally developed an understanding of it. In fact, he believed that children do not *learn* cognitive lessons from toys, but instead use them to assimilate concepts they've already developed. It didn't take long, however, for American parents and so-called experts to turn his model on its head. Toy advertisements and child-development manuals rushed to offer lots of advice on how parents could coach their kids through the Piagetian stages. Consider this advice, for instance, claiming to encourage parenting à la Piaget:

> Your [eight- to twelve-month-old] child may now be ready for more advanced games in his search for the hidden object. If he has learned to find a toy that he watched you hide under one cover, try using two covers such as a diaper and a towel. Be sure they are unpatterned and plain enough so you know the baby is reaching for the toy and not for the covering. . . . When your baby is consistently successful at this game, try it with three covers—say, a diaper, a towel, and a cushion.
>
> —*Your Baby's Mind and How it Grows: Piaget's Theory for Parents,* by Mary Ann Spencer Pulaski, 1978

Pity the poor baby whose parents are so busy putting him through his Piagetian paces that he gets little chance to actually *play.* Unstructured time with a responsive adult is baby's real chance to explore and test reality on his own initiative. Pat Belby is director of the employees' child-care center, at Little Tikes, where the company regularly tests its toys. She believes one of the benefits of unstructured play is that it gives a child the freedom to learn for himself: "Sometimes parents try to take charge too quickly, instead of allowing a lull to let the child formulate the idea in her mind and let it gel," she says. In succumbing to the hype that would have had poor misunderstood Piaget tearing his hair out in exasperation, parents are depriving their kids of the chance to discover the world independently. According to

Belby, the mistake can be simply stated: "Parent intervention is often too soon and too strong."

Ironically, the would-be Piagetians are joined in their highly serious approach to the power of toys by another group of "experts" who don't think parents need to teach but believe toys can do it all. If would-be Piagetian parents view themselves as cognitive coaches whose practice sessions require the right toys, those who follow the Montessori method have gone one step further. For them, the right toys can teach a child everything, from math to reading. By the 1960s, many parents were taking Maria Montessori's slogan "Play is a child's work" as an invitation to switch their kids from hide-and-seek to hard labor. In Montessori's method, every toy (or "didactic material") is designed to teach a specific lesson—no less and no more. "Our didactic material renders auto-education possible, permits a methodical education of the senses," writes Montessori in *The Montessori Method* (1912). "Not upon the ability of the teacher does such education rest, but upon the didactic system."

One of Montessori's didactic materials, for example, consists of a series of ten cubes, precisely described: "The first has a base of ten centimeters, and the others decrease, successively, one centimeter as to base, the smallest cube having a base of one centimetre." The didactic exercise entails "throwing the cubes, which are pink in colour, down upon a green carpet, and then building them up into a little tower, placing the largest cube as the base, and then placing the others in order of size until the little cube of one centimetre is placed at the top." Clearly the child who would prefer to build a firehouse or a castle with his cubes is in deep trouble.

Then there's Montessori's series of ten rods, ranging from ten centimeters to a meter in length, each with colored markings. "The child arranges the rods which have first been scattered and mixed," explains Montessori. "He puts them together according to the gradation of length, and observes the correspondence of colours. . . . This most important set of blocks will have its principal application in arithmetic, as we shall see." Needless to say, the child is *not* supposed to choose one or two rods and pull them along the floor while making the *"vroom-vroom"* noise. Forget fun. Forget imagination. What every child needs is a set of toys cleverly designed to impart every cognitive skill under the sun.

And the "experts" have lost no time in seeing Montessori methodology in every toy on the market. Who cares whether or not a toy is appealing to your particular child, or whether he happens to take a fancy to it? Certain toys *must* be played with; otherwise, Very Important Skills will fail to develop later on. Take the simple pegboard, for instance. "The peg toy is the forerunner of shape-discrimination toys (such as shape sorters and jigsaw puzzles)," writes Athina Aston soberly in *Toys that Teach Your Child from Birth to Two* (1904), "and the skill it develops is the first of progressively more complex perceptual skills which culminate in the child's ability to read." To call a pegboard simple, it seems, is not only to misunderstand but to insult its marvelous didactic powers.

No wonder the toy merchandisers get away with such extravagant claims. Why, every toy on the shelf is a potential Mary Poppins and Mr. Chips waiting to be let loose on *your* little bundle of IQ points! One popular catalog even notes the "educational play value" of each toy, implying that every toy effortlessly imparts specific cognitive skills—from matching and sorting to language development and problem-solving. Take a helicopter-shaped teether, for example, imported from England and described as follows: "Educational Play Value: Teething, two-handed coordination, eye-hand coordination, object constancy." (Heaven forbid the poor infant should merely soothe his sore gums!)

Let's face it, if knowledge were actually *built into* objects, most of us would be able to clean up our desks merely by purchasing an in-box and an out-box. Unfortunately for the toy merchandisers (and parents who spend their hard-earned money on toys advertised as miracle workers), learning is considerably more complicated.

Do Toys Really Teach Anything, and If So, What?

Now let's go back to our second question: Do our kids really need all this stuff? Is there any evidence that educational toys actually *teach* kids anything? Louise Bates Ames, the cofounder and associate director of the Gesell Institute in New Haven, Connecticut, thinks not. "I believe in the mind, and I like bright kids," she says, "but by now I have great-grandchildren, and I don't buy educational toys as such. Blocks are always good, puzzles are always good—all the things we've *always* bought children are good—but you don't have to buy special educational toys."

Two researchers at Florida State University analyzed the homes of preschool children who scored high on various cognitive-ability tests and tried to determine which types of toys and play materials were commonly available to them. What they discovered, as they reported in 1985, was that children who were rated as highly verbal, who had good quantitative skills, or good memories tended to own structured toys, such as puzzles. The same toys were also found in the homes of children who scored high on perceptual-performance tests, along with *fluid* materials (such as paint and clay) and *microsymbolic* toys (hand-held miniatures of real objects, such as cars, trucks, and farm animals). But the researchers are careful to state, the children's ages and socio-economic status were also important factors in the development of all these skills. Moreover, it's the type of *play* that is encouraged that's the important thing, not mere toy ownership. And that depends more on encouragement from Mom and Dad than on having the right toy. "It must . . . be acknowledged that measures based solely on the number of toys in the home are indirect. The conclusion that the interaction of child and parents is involved and must be directly observed seems inescapable," write the researchers. "Future research in this area should include in-home observations of how the toys are really used during play and what parents do to facilitate or hamper cognitive development as they interact with their child."

And in fact, despite the Montessori claim that toys (or "didactic materials") can stimulate "auto-education," most studies emphasize *play* rather than toys as a means to learning. And even on that point there's plenty of debate.

Play's the Thing

One of the main problems with highly structured educational toys is that they seem to bring out the inflexible, goal-oriented beast inside every parent. As Bruno Bettelheim writes in *A Good Enough Parent* (1987), "Educational toys become absolutely deadly when the child is expected to learn what they are designed to teach rather than what he wants to learn." It used to bother me that my son, as a toddler, refused to use his shape sorter "properly" by fitting the shapes—triangle, circle, and square—through the appropriate cutouts in the lid. Instead, he insisted on taking off the lid and putting the shapes inside so that he could stir them with a toy spoon, "cooking dinner," as he explained. Now, I had paid eleven dollars for this shape sorter, and here he was using it like any wooden spoon and mixing bowl I could have lent him from the kitchen for free! So convinced was I that there was only one way he would learn anything from this toy that I *taped the lid shut* to force him to use the holes.

Guess what? I was an idiot. He was *playing,* learning what he wanted to learn instead of what I and my expensive shape sorter were determined to teach.

Developmental psychologists have generated enough scholarly articles on the subject of play to paper the walls of every preschool in America. Yet they still haven't agreed on what children learn from play, how they learn it, or even what play is. Many do concur on one point, though: adult-directed, goal-oriented activities are everything that true play is *not.* Playing is something a child spontaneously does of his own accord, and (with the exception of block-building, which is usually goal-oriented) it focuses on the means rather than the end. No matter how much fun you think your child is having when you're making a game out of drilling him on his carefully selected alphabet blocks, he's not playing. (This is not to say he isn't learning from your drill, but he'll learn other things from play that you can't teach him.) And contrary to what you might conclude by reading some of the development charts, play varies in nature from child to child, from situation to situation.

Surprisingly enough, true play does not necessarily involve toys at all. Scientists are only beginning to study language play, for example, but you've probably already noticed this phenomenon as your preschooler experiments with rhymes, funny-sounding words, maybe even a made-up language. Objects are not the originators of play, *children* are. In fact, psychologists draw a distinction between "exploratory behavior" and play by noting that the playful child holding a toy or household object does not so much seem to wonder, What is this thing and what can it do? as What can I do with this thing? I saw a vivid example of this one day in an upholstery shop, where the three-year-old son of the owner was entertaining himself with a pair of scissors and a few scraps of fabric. He carefully snipped at a square of material for a while, making several holes. Then he held it up triumphantly: "A fire engine!" he proclaimed. And he spent a good quarter hour absorbed in "driving" it around the bolts of fabric, making loud *"zooms"* and siren sounds.

But so what? Who says play does young children any good, anyway? Aren't they better off—considering how little they know—learning something about the real world with a knowledgeable adult as teacher? Or at least playing only with educational toys designed to teach them something? Maria Montessori vigorously espoused this point of view in *The Secret of Childhood* (1966).

A child is taught to see horses, castles, or trains in the bricks and blocks that he arranges in various ways. A child's imagination can give a symbolic meaning to any object whatever, but this creates fantastic mirages within his mind. A knob becomes a horse, a chair a throne, a stone an airplane.

Children are given toys with which they can play, but which create illusions and afford no real and productive contact with reality.

Though Montessori's disapproval of pretend play derived from her respect for children's ability and desire to learn, she was in fact underestimating the range and importance of human playfulness. Many experts believe that fantasy or pretend play—say, making believe that a chair is a spaceship, or a bar of soap is a doll's dinner—develops not only a child's imagination but also some important cognitive concepts. Pretend play, according to these theorists, is a child's first encounter with *symbolic thinking,* the idea that one object can stand for another. At first a child is unable to imagine an object, such as a horse, without seeing it. But during pretend play, he takes a first step toward doing so, using a concrete object (such as a stick to represent a horse) as a prop. The concrete object, which in early stages of pretend play physically resembles the imagined object (a hat for a boat, for example) functions as a "pivot," or substitute for the imagined object. Eventually the child will be able to imagine an object without the use of the pivot—to fantasize about horses without even having a stick to ride. This is his introduction to abstract thought, the world beyond what he can see and touch. In time he will feel equally comfortable with more sophisticated concepts: that the letters *C-A-T* represent his favorite feline, for example; or that the earth is round.

Researchers have also pointed to a link between playfulness and creativity. One 1969 study found a group of children from Montessori schools (which use highly structured materials designed to teach a specific lesson) to be *less creative* than children from traditional nursery schools. The discoveries that take place with less structured materials (paint, water, blocks, and household junk) seem to carry over into many other spheres of learning.

As Erik Erikson points out in *Toys and Reasons* (1977), there is a joyous quality to spontaneous play that can permeate every aspect of life: ". . . If play so obviously helps the exercise of growing faculties, it does so with inventiveness and abandon . . . Unimpaired playfulness . . . not only endows events categorized as play; it is so much a part of being active and alive that it soon tends to elude any definition . . ."

Piaget, in his classic study *Play, Dreams and Imitation in Childhood* (1962), also notes that children are motivated to play for the pleasure of it, a phenomenon which is inseparable from learning.

> After learning to grasp, swing, throw, etc., which involve both an effort of accommodation to new situations, and an effort of repetition, reproduction and generalisation, which are the elements of assimilation, the child sooner or later (often even during the learning period) grasps for the pleasure of grasping, swings for the sake of swinging, etc. In a word, he repeats his behaviour not in any further effort to learn or to investigate, but for the mere joy of mastering it and of showing off to himself his own power of subduing reality.

A child whose playfulness is encouraged is likely to grow up, like Curious George, with an insatiable desire to learn about his world and everything in it. But even without encouragement, children are naturally motivated to play because play—unstructured and seemingly without purpose—is a powerful stimulant; it cures boredom. Simply put, when their environment fails to provide them with entertainment, children find a way to amuse themselves—like the boy cutting a "fire engine" out of fabric in the upholstery shop. Children who become adept at this have the opportunity to develop what Bettelheim calls a "rich inner life" and virtually never complain, "Mommy, there's nothing to do." But if kids are constantly supervised, organized, and structured by parents who insist on getting their money's worth out of a collection of the "right" toys to be used in the "right" way, how do they learn to truly play? "It is amazing what an infant can learn just by playing with the cardboard core of a roll of toilet paper," says Bettelheim, "and how constructive, imaginative, and educative a child's play with empty boxes can be."

In fact, a number of studies show that children may actually learn *more* when left to their own devices and allowed to explore a toy's possibilities than they do when taught the "right" way to play with it. Such learning can include important life lessons, like the value of persistence. When a block tower topples, a child at play learns that he can eventually find a way to make it stand if he will try, try again. If we only offer praise for clear-cut success and right answers—threading the red spool onto the red post, or fitting the triangle into the triangular hole—we are failing to encourage our kids to learn through open-ended experiment. When, on the contrary, we express support for effort, creativity, and curiosity, we are fostering a love of learning and a willingness to try even when success is not assured.

Problem-solving ability also seems to be fostered through free play. In one 1976 study, preschool children were given a problem to solve in the form of a prize that was out of reach. To get it, they had to clamp two sticks together and use the combined length to rake the prize toward them. The children were split into three groups. The training group was shown the whole solution. A second group had free play with the sticks and clamps, and the third (the control group), no treatment at all. As they tried to solve the problem, the children were given a standardized series of hints. The children in the play group did as well at solving the problem as the group that had actually observed the solution, and they did much better than the control group. Interestingly enough, the children in the play group were observed to be *more goal-directed and more persistent* than their counterparts in the other two groups. Subsequent experiments have shown that the children with the free-play experience actually perform *better* than the training group, both in terms of solution time and in the number of required hints.

Finally, it's important to keep in mind that there is more to play than cognitive learning. When your child plays with other children, of course, he is learning to share, to take turns, and to enjoy being with others. All of these lessons are important preparation for life in the adult worlds of family and work. Likewise, when your child is dressing up in your shoes, or pretending to mop the kitchen floor, he is rehearsing his future roles as a functional member of society and home. A 1982 study at the University of North Carolina showed that children who were encouraged to imitate their parents by playing at household chores, such as sweeping and dusting, tended to want to "help" more. When your child picks up a stick and pretends to vacuum the living room, keep in mind that with a few pats on the back from you, he may be willing to help with the housework as he gets older.

Healthy Ways to Help

Most child-development books include a list of "age-appropriate toys" that conscientious parents can go out and buy to shore up their child's intellect. The authors are hoping not that readers will buy out their local toy store, but that the various playthings will encourage them to spend time with their child and encourage the child to learn and explore his world. Of course, the toy merchandisers who sell the fourteen-page activity booklets along with their products know this, too. As Pat Belby of Little Tikes puts it, "A key to a good toy is that it has not only child appeal, but parent appeal also. If the parent is attracted to the toy and feels real positive toward the toy, there's going to be some pleasant interaction." In fact, says Belby, most toy manufacturers realize that parents are often really buying the toys for *themselves,* not their kids. "Something that *they* might have liked to have is what they often buy," says Belby. "I think that's the way a lot of toys are sold. We have a generation of parents who can afford to buy things they may have wished for when they were kids."

Besides, let's face it, a home filled with discarded egg cartons, old appliance boxes, and empty containers from the kitchen might delight your child, but it doesn't exactly look like *House*

Beautiful. So instead, your child's playroom features a miniature version of your dream kitchen, a grocery store stocked with everything but fish on ice, and several garages filled with trucks and cars in every model Detroit, Japan, and West Germany can produce. If so, you're not alone: according to one study, American children spend three times as many hours per day playing with realistic toys as they do playing with household objects not specifically designed as playthings.

Will it surprise you to learn that this expensive investment in kids' imaginations probably *isn't* doing much for them? In fact, research shows that a *mixture* of "low-realism" and "high-realism" toys stimulates children's imaginations most effectively. Younger preschoolers do seem to engage in more fantasy play when they have realistic toys—vehicles clearly designed to be garbage trucks or ambulances, or plastic food that looks like the real thing. But as they get older, such toys actually *limit* their creativity. Low-realism props, however, such as simple toys and junk—anything, from old socks to cigar boxes—enrich play at any age. Let your child get his hands on the nonbreakable household items he's probably begging to play with anyway, and his imagination will soar.

Imagine all the grown-up toys you could buy for *yourself* if you weren't dropping so many paychecks at Child World and Toys R Us! That's why, in this book, I'm *not* going to offer the usual chart of age-appropriate toys designed to send you back to the toy store every six to eight weeks. Instead, on the premise that it is not the *toy* that defines the play, but the *child,* I'm offering a list of ten basic toys that will *grow with your child* all through the preschool years. Give him the same toy at age six months, one year, two years, and so on, and he will play with it differently.

Many parents who went crazy buying "age-appropriate" toys for their firstborn make a surprising discovery when baby number two comes along: toys have a much longer useful life than the manufacturers would like us to think! My son, Matthew, had virtually every educational toy right on schedule. His sister, Laura, on the other hand, doesn't know what she's supposed to like, and from five months on, she's been in love with a wooden train set. She began by mouthing the cars, and now (at eight months) she runs them across the floor. Admittedly, you'll want to pick up a new puzzle from time to time as your child's skills increase, but otherwise all you need to supplement this list is the occasional household item (see note at end). *You're* likely to get sick of these toys long before your child.

The Only Ten Toys Your Child Really Needs

1. Unit, or "kindergarten," blocks. "Nobody wants blocks anymore," my local educational-toy store owner told me sadly when I asked why he'd let his stock run low. "They only want to buy toys they think their kids will learn something from." As educators have been telling us for decades, blocks provide endless opportunities for learning at virtually every age. Hardwood blocks with beveled edges (for safety's sake) are the classics, although Duplo and hollow cardboard blocks are also great.

Remember the poem "Block City" in Robert Louis Stevenson's *A Child's Garden of Verses?* It gives a wonderful child's-eye view of the way blocks make a child feel like the master of his universe:

What are you able to build with your blocks?
Castles and palaces, temples and docks.
Rain may keep raining, and others go roam,
But I can be happy and building at home.

Let the sofa be mountains, the carpet be sea,
There I'll establish a city for me:
A kirk and a mill and a palace beside,
And a harbor as well where my vessels may ride. . . .

Unlike, say, doing a "math-readiness" workbook, block play is an immediate, tactile experience. In his autobiography, Frank

Lloyd Wright recalls the experience of playing with kindergarten blocks in the 1870s as one of the influences that led him to become an architect. "The smooth, shapely maple blocks with which to build," he writes, "the sense of which never afterwards left the fingers: so form became feeling."

Blocks, simple as they are, offer a wealth of possibilities for children:

- Newborns enjoy hearing Mom or Dad bang two of them together.

- Older babies enjoy manipulating blocks and knocking down towers that parents (and siblings, especially) build.

- Toddlers feel important carrying around blocks and making piles of them.

- Young preschoolers build low constructions and begin to make patterns.

- Threes and fours build bridges, then enclosures, then balanced and decorative patterns, often incorporating other toys (dolls, play people, and animals) as well as items from around the house (spools, containers, bits of fabric, and styrofoam); they also begin naming their creations.

- As they play with blocks, children get hands-on experience with mathematical concepts such as shape, weight, thickness, width, length, and balance. They begin to acquire a genuine concept of number, which is far more useful than learning to rattle off the numbers from one to fifty. When a preschool child takes his blocks off the shelf and has them spread out on the floor, he thinks he now has more blocks. With time and experience he learns otherwise.

2. Boxes and containers (preferably with lids, such as yogurt or pint-size ice-cream containers) in different sizes.

■ For a newborn, you can fill a small cup with beans, snap on a lid, and then tie it to his wrist to use as a rattle. Or tie a few onto the infant seat—a three-month-old will enjoy swiping at them.

■ Fill a medium-sized container, such as an oatmeal box, with a few household items (be sure they're not choking hazards) and watch your older baby empty it. Later on, he'll learn to refill it himself. He'll also use it as a drum.

■ The young toddler will practice using a set of various-sized cups (such as measuring cups) as nesting toys, or use them to feed his doll.

■ As children begin to play together, around the age of three, they can have "tea parties" using containers as teacups.

3. Small Vehicles. A few different sizes are nice to have, preferably at least one car and one truck. Ideally, one of the vehicles should have an open door or window, and a working trunk or liftgate, allowing the older child to insert a driver or cargo.

■ Babies will enjoy grasping smaller cars. Once they can sit up, they'll keep busy spinning the wheels, and soon they're running the vehicles across the floor.

■ Toddlers have great fun making the *"vroom-vroom!"* noise as they race their cars and trucks around the house. Tie a string to a stable, not-too-heavy car and it's a pull-toy. Show them how to put the vehicles back in the box when playtime is over.

■ Preschoolers may use the box as a bridge, or build a road or racetrack with blocks and run their vehicles along that.

Small figures will serve as drivers, and household objects (from pencils to quarters) can be loaded on as logs or other cargo. Help your child hook a few together with pipe cleaners, and he's got a train.

4. Riding Toy. Forget the battery-powered models and choose a simple car or trike that runs by kid power, which is one resource we all have in abundance!

■ A toddler who's still unsteady on his feet can walk behind a car and push it along. Tie on some bells and it's even more fun.

■ An older toddler will enjoy riding along. He's too young to pedal, but he can pull himself with his feet on the ground.

■ Preschoolers love to build up speed as they pedal down driveways (or hallways). Riding toys become a favorite part of pretend play, too; they can be cars bringing groceries home, dune buggies, trucks that carry rocks around the yard—whatever.

5. Doll or play-figure family Both boys and girls find a multitude of uses for small figures, whether they're Raggedy Andy, He-Man, baby dolls that squeak when squeezed, or Duplo people.

■ Babies get excited when Mom and Dad squeak dolls for them. Small figures that aren't choking hazards are just the thing for grasping "practice." And a doll often becomes a "cuddly," or beloved object that gets dragged everywhere.

■ Toddlers will tuck their dolls into bed or feed them dinner—first signs of pretend play.

■ Preschoolers often incorporate dolls into block play ("Look, Mom—he's climbing up the side of the building!"), and who could be a better companion for fantasy play?

6. *Ball.* As a practical matter, you will probably need several different balls to suit your developing child and your play environment. An infant may enjoy a "clutch" ball that has hollows he can grasp. A toddler who is beginning to practice throwing will do better with a slightly larger ball; likewise preschoolers who are learning to catch. However, if you'll be playing indoors (especially in a room with windows), your best bet is a nice soft beach ball.

■ A baby who has learned to sit will enjoy rolling a ball back and forth.

■ An infant who crawls has a great time chasing a ball.

■ Toddlers begin to learn how to throw, although with rather erratic aim. You can catch the ball or provide large targets— a string to throw it over, a basketball hoop that attaches to the furniture, or a few bowling pins (old plastic baby bottles work fine).

7. *Puzzles.* Your child's toddler puzzle will be too easy to be used for its original purpose as he gets older, but you can put it to many more uses. The pieces in wooden puzzles with pegs can be used by preschoolers as stand-up toys. In fact, if you buy one when your child is still an infant, he will enjoy grasping and examining the pieces (as long as the pieces are not small enough to be choking hazards, and the pegs are securely attached). Some three- and four-year-olds enjoy tracing toddler puzzle pieces with crayons.

When you're looking for puzzles for your preschooler, keep in mind that doing the same one repeatedly gets boring. There are inexpensive do-it-yourself puzzles on the market that consist of blank jigsaws on which you glue or draw any picture you think your child will find appealing. And there are also puzzle games and play tiles that use the same set of geometric shapes to create a wide variety of pictures and give your child the opportunity to design his own as well.

8. *Pail and shovel.* Not to be relegated to beach use only, these are inexpensive and versatile for year-round play.

■ A young baby can grasp the shovel and chew on it.

■ Older babies are devoted packrats. Fill a pail with a collection of household items, and your eight-month-old will practice emptying it. Later on, he'll practice filling it, too. He may try to imitate you if you "play the drum" by turning the pail upside down and banging on it with the shovel. And be sure to try bringing it into the tub at bathtime.

■ A toddler will be delighted to stand at the sink and fill and empty his pail. If you're not in the mood for a mop-up, you can put the pail in a large cardboard box filled with oatmeal or rice and let him use that instead.

■ For a preschooler, pretending can turn a pail and shovel into anything: a pail might be a hat or a cake-mixing bowl, and a shovel anything from a baseball bat to a microphone.

9. *Xylophone with mallet.* If you're lucky enough to have a piano at home, that's even better. Otherwise, any toy instrument you can find that plays different tones will provide a young child with an enjoyable introduction to music-making.

■ A very young baby will take pleasure in hearing you play.

■ Your older baby may hit the keys, first with his hands, then with the mallet.

■ Toddlers love to parade around while playing music. For this purpose, the inexpensive xylophone pull-toy marketed by Fisher-Price is hard to beat.

89

■ Your preschooler may be interested in learning to play a song, whether it's one he makes up or a tune you teach him.

10. Art supplies. Without spending much money, you can assemble a variety of materials—crayons, paints, brushes, glue, paper, and play dough—that will give your child the opportunity to have fun through creative expression. Those high-priced easels sold by educational toy companies are appealing, but your child can also stand up and paint if you tape the paper to a wall. Some kids, like my son, actually prefer to sit down, no matter what the child-development books recommend. Help yours keep the paper in one place by taping it to the table.

Save paper bags to make puppets; pasta, cotton balls, and styrofoam packing "peanuts" for collages; and sponges, leaves, paper clips, potatoes, and other items with interesting textures to make prints and rubbings. And, of course, be sure to start a gallery showing your child's creations on your refrigerator.

■ Toddlers are just learning to hold a crayon. Making marks on a page makes them feel important. Many of them begin to learn their colors. Provided they don't eat it, they can have fun manipulating playdough.

■ Preschoolers enjoy the process of putting color on a page. "Process, not product," is the preschooler's motto. Their idea of drawing a bird may be hopping the crayon across the page, making "tracks." Many will begin to draw stick figures, though. And when they're not feeling artistic, they can use their drawing materials in pretend play—crayons make good cargo loaded onto the back of a truck, or doll barbells, or candles stuck into Play-Doh for a "birthday cake."

Household Objects are also fun for a baby to manipulate or a preschooler to use in pretend play. The only criterion is safety: give him plastic or paper plates, buttons (strung on a cord at first, later in a jar), dress-up clothes, an old suitcase, shoeboxes, old oven mitts, pots and pans, safe kitchen tools (broom, rake, shovel, mop, rolling pin), empty food cans, jars with the labels on, and so forth.

Don't worry that you need to offer your baby *all* of these items. There's no point in replacing the frantic search for the "right" educational toy with an equally frantic search for the ideal collection of simple playthings. As most parents find out, children have a way of finding household objects that interest them with no help at all from us! And it's that same natural urge to discover and explore that motivates them to learn from even the simplest, most "unscientific" toys. Most important, of course, is *what* they learn. The educational toy promoters (both authors and advertisers) have emphasized cognitive learning and motor skills as by-products of play. But as he plays, alone and with others, your child is developing both emotionally and socially as well. That's why play needs to be fun. By letting him take the lead, encouraging his curiosity and fantasy, and showing that you really enjoy his company, you're helping him build self-esteem and setting a pattern for healthy human relationships. No toy can do that.

Today's Nursery Schools: Where Ivy League Meets Ivory Snow

"I take parents around the school, and one of the first questions they ask me—and these are parents of prospective two-year-olds—is, 'Where do children from here usually go to college?' I think everyone is just getting so worried."
—*Margaret Bloodgood, admissions director, The City and Country School, New York City*

NOT LONG AGO a man in his sixties told me how surprised he was to hear that his two-year-old granddaughter was going off to preschool. "I can remember when my kids were young, the big question among all the young couples was whether it was right to send your *four-*year-old to nursery school," he said, shaking his head. "Now it seems as though the earlier the better. Heaven forbid they should waste time at home *playing!*"

Today, according to the National Center for Education Statistics, 64 percent of preschoolers whose family incomes are over twenty thousand dollars a year attend nursery school. Sixty-eight percent of college graduates with children between the ages of three and five send them to preschool. Nursery or preschool has apparently become such a widely accepted part of the typical American middle-class child's life that in 1987 two of the major parenting magazines ran first-person accounts by mothers explaining why they dared to be revolutionary and let their three-year-olds languish at home. "By not enrolling [Kate] in a structured preschool program, I deliberately denied her something that most of her little friends will have: a 14th year in the classroom before she finishes high school," wrote Ann Banks in *Parenting.* "I wanted Kate to be with other children, but I despaired of ever finding a freewheeling, imaginative environment for her. It seemed that my values conflicted with the prevailing parental philosophy. What many parents appeared to regard as an appropriate level of socialization . . . I thought of as being prematurely broken to the harness."

What's more, many of today's preschools are a far cry from the ones we attended as kids, where a few hours of fun, finger painting, and the occasional caged rabbit were considered enrichment enough. If it's not academic—if it doesn't offer a child a head start on those all-important numbers and letters—it's not worth the tuition fee. As the columnist Anna Quindlen wrote in the *New York Times,* " 'It's a sweet, traditional little school,' someone told me about one institution, explaining, I must add, why some parents were dissatisfied with it. Can you imagine being foolish enough to send your child to a sweet, traditional little school? He might turn out to be a sweet, traditional little person."

We've come a long way since 1837, when Friedrich Froebel founded the first kindergarten as a real "garden for children" where kids were meant to learn and develop naturally through play. These days many parents seem to view nursery school as designed to get kids ready to read by kindergarten—if they haven't been smart enough to learn before that. Many parents are urging public school administrators to admit four-year-olds to kindergarten, and schools like the Sylvan Learning Center and

Reading Game are setting up pricey tutoring programs to help four- and five-year-olds work on their reading and math. And all too often, preschool directors who know which side their bread is buttered on are giving unsuspecting kids just what their parents are asking for.

It's a trend that has its roots in the years between World Wars I and II, when Maria Montessori's approach to education set the tone for the growing nursery-school movement. During this period, children were expected to learn to do a great deal for themselves, according to Christina Hardyment, the author of *Dream Babies* (1983), a history of child-care advice in Britain and the United States: "The central idea of the Montessori system was self-education. . . . Its purpose was to teach the child how to cope more competently with life."

As family size decreased, and as the popularity of Montessori's methods grew, children were often packed off to nursery school by the age of two or three. During the Depression of the thirties, emergency nursery schools were set up to create jobs for teachers and nurses who were out of work, and to help needy parents provide food and safe amusement for their children. During World War II, as both mothers and fathers took part in the war effort, nursery school and federally funded day-care facilities met a demand for child care. "We had two-year-olds during World War II," notes Margaret Bloodgood of the City and Country School, "because it was needed then."

Today, preschools are one answer to families' needs in a more hectic, less friendly world than we grew up in. With two thirds of preschoolers' mothers employed outside the home, kids don't seem to wander in and out of each other's houses the way they did in the days of Wally and the Beaver. Preschool is one safe place to make friends. "It's a necessity," says Bloodgood. "People don't make friends that much at the park. . . . There aren't necessarily other children in one's [apartment] building or next door. So to have time for children to be with other children, you have to fix it up. It can't just happen anymore."

To meet the needs of employed parents, many programs offer extended child-care schedules from early morning to late evening. It's not uncommon for parents to refer to these day-care programs as "school." And during the long day at the center, parents want evidence that their kids are being "stimulated" through a variety of programmed activities. Small wonder that some teachers are sending them home with dittoed worksheets. As the National Association for the Education of Young Children (NAEYC) noted with dismay in its position paper *Good Teaching Practices for 4- and 5-Year-Olds,* there is

> increasingly widespread demand for use of inappropriate formal teaching techniques for young children [and] overemphasis on achievement of narrowly defined academic skills . . . These trends are primarily the result of misconceptions about how young children learn . . . In many cases, concerned adults, who want children to succeed, apply adult education standards to the curriculum for young children and pressure early-childhood programs to demonstrate that children are 'really learning.'

As you visit the "traditional" nursery schools, with their blocks, paint, and sand tables, they may pale in comparison to programs that promise to "let your child's intellect soar," as one school in my area advertises. It's easy to be dazzled by a name or philosophy without really considering how a particular program works in *practice,* or whether it's really suited to your child's temperament or stage of development. So what happens? You decide on the school with the slickest brochure—the one that makes promises designed to appeal to success-oriented parents with big bank accounts. You plunk down more of your hard-earned money for tuition payments than you need to, and your child ends up feeling pushed instead of playful. It's hard to imagine that this state of affairs could continue if more parents knew what the research by early-childhood specialists really shows about preschool education—what it can accomplish for kids and what it can't. That's what this chapter is all about.

A Head Start on Harvard?

Study after study tells us that preschool education is a good way to prevent a child from failing later on in school. How tempting it is to conclude that therefore more is better—that the more "academic" and "advanced" the program, the better it will prepare your child for school. Not so fast. A look at what the studies say about *which* children benefit most from preschool, *what* they seem to learn, and *how* they learn will yield a few surprises.

One of the strongest sources of support for the idea that preschool is effective with *disadvantaged* children is the well-known Perry Preschool project in Michigan, a High/Scope Educational Research Foundation study that followed 123 poor black children with low IQs over a twenty-two-year period. At ages three and four the children were split into two groups; one attended the Perry Preschool and the other didn't. At age nineteen, those enrolled in the preschool program were more likely to be literate, employed, and enrolled in college or vocational school. Among that group there were fewer school dropouts, teenage mothers, and welfare recipients, and fewer had been labeled mentally retarded or arrested for delinquency. The study provides a great deal of information of interest to educators, legislators, and taxpayers. But it tells us absolutely nothing about the SAT scores of middle-class kids who've been to nursery school. That wasn't its purpose.

Head Start is a similar example of a program whose results are often cited as evidence that preschool "works." Yet it's important to remember that, as part of Lyndon Johnson's War on Poverty, Head Start was conceived as a *comprehensive* early intervention for poor children, designed not only to focus on cognitive development but on the child's social, emotional, and physical health as well. Head Start began as a series of short summer sessions, but by 1972 it ran all year round. Since that time, it's been studied literally hundreds of times, so it's not surprising that misinformation about it is as widespread as the common cold in a nursery-school class in January. But parents who think Head Start provides any evidence that preschools can create superbabies would do well to consider two critical facts about the program:

1. Head Start does not seem to increase children's cognitive skills over the long term. Although Head Start children show significant gains on intelligence tests while they are enrolled in the program and immediately afterward, they don't seem to stay that way. As the children progress through school, few studies have found differences between them and their non-Head Start peers on achievement tests. "One year after Head Start, the differences between Head Start and non-Head Start children on achievement and school readiness tests continue to be in the educationally meaningful range, but the two groups score at about the same level on intelligence tests," notes the bureau's pamphlet entitled *The Impact of Head Start on Children, Families and Communities.* "By the end of the second year there are no educationally meaningful differences on any of the measures."

Several studies do show that Head Start kids are less likely to be "left back" in school, or become dropouts. Researchers conclude that these factors relate not only to academic achievement but also to social competence, which Head Start may well promote.

2. *Head Start children do not, on the average, catch up with their middle-class counterparts.* A 1974 study of 248 children in the Hartford, Connecticut, public schools found that kids who participated in Head Start gained an average of thirteen months in mental age but remained eight months below norms.

Apparently a few hours a day spent in preschool—no matter how good the program is—cannot make up for the deprivation these children suffer for the rest of the day. Keep in mind that according to a 1980 study, 72 percent of their families used food stamps and 66 percent were on welfare. Many lacked the health care their middle-class counterparts enjoyed; a 1970 study of one Head Start center found that 34 percent had not seen a physician in two years, and half had not been immunized against childhood diseases.

As for studies of what preschool attendance does for children who are *not* poor, there isn't much out there. But the Brookline Early Education Project (BEEP) in Massachusetts did find that, after a developmentally appropriate five-year program, middle-class children seemed to have fewer school problems than their counterparts who did not participate. By the end of the second grade, 14 percent of BEEP's middle-class participants exhibited inappropriate classroom learning behavior—half as many as the control group—and 19 percent had reading problems, as opposed to 32 percent of the control group. Not as dramatic a contrast as those in the studies of poor children, but a clear indication that a good preschool program can help a child handle academics when the time comes.

A Chicago study compared eighty children aged two and three on measures of "developmental competencies," such as cognitive ability, social knowledge, and sociability with an adult stranger, and found that nursery-school kids came out on top. But the researchers point out that the parents who put their children in nursery school were themselves the most highly educated. Preschool was just one part of their children's total milieu.

Name-Brand Nursery Schools?

Suzuki? Montessori? Piaget-inspired? If you're used to shopping for designer labels, it's easy to get caught up in the names and methods attached to today's trendiest preschools. It's hard to find a program these days that bills itself as merely "warm and loving"—"challenging" and "stimulating" are the name of the game. Yet study after study shows that although highly academic programs—the kind that emphasize numbers and letters—often produce impressive results in the short term, as children grow and progress through school the differences disappear.

In fact, *there is no evidence that ANY one preschool teaching method produces a brighter child than the next.* In 1986, for example, the High/Scope Educational Research Foundation reported on its long-term Preschool Curriculum Comparison study. Researchers traced the effects of three different types of preschool approaches on sixty-eight poor children in Michigan through age fifteen. They named and defined these approaches as follows:

- *Direct instruction*—a teacher-directed approach in which children are taught language, reading, and arithmetic (The Suzuki method is a well-known example, as are Glenn Doman's Better Baby Institute programs.)

- *Nursery school*—a traditional approach, with children allowed to initiate their own activities in the classroom's various play areas, and the teacher interfering very little except for safety purposes

- *High/Scope curriculum*—an approach in which kids initiated their own activities but the teacher maintained a more active role than in the traditional nursery setting, by arranging the room to promote learning and by making plans and reviewing the children's activities with them ("What are you going to build with your blocks?" "Gee, that purple block is even brighter than that yellow one, isn't it?")

What did the researchers conclude about the relative merits of the three different approaches? In terms of cognitive development, the Direct Instruction group showed a temporary IQ advantage over the other two at the end of the program, *but did not significantly differ in their IQs and school achievement scores at any other*

99

time. At age fifteen there was one interesting difference between the direct instruction group and the other two, however: the direct instruction "graduates" reported having committed twice as many delinquent acts as their Nursery and High/Scope counterparts. The latter two each reported having committed only about one fifth as many acts of property violence as the direct instruction group and about half as many acts of personal violence, drug abuse, and in-family offenses.

How do child-development experts explain this? Lawrence J. Schweinhart of the High/Scope Educational Research Foundation suggests that the more structured programs' short-term gains "may simply be an adult-satisfying diversion from the need to focus on conversational language, personal responsibility for learning, and other developmentally important skills and dispositions." As he sees it, by spending so much time and energy on teaching children instead of giving them an opportunity to learn for themselves, the highly structured programs actually *deprive* children: "The direct instruction preschool program may have failed to take full advantage of the opportunities that were available to positively influence the development of young children's social problem-solving skills." Perhaps, he suggests, voicing an opinion shared by many early-childhood experts, preschoolers are at a critical age for the acquisition of these skills, while the academic kind can be learned later.

One Man's Montessori Is Another Man's Piaget

The High/Scope researchers in the above study chose three labels for the kinds of preschool programs they were examining. But keep in mind that names don't mean much. Your local "traditional" nursery school may be using techniques similar to the so-called High/Scope curriculum—letting the kids take the lead in planning their activities, but challenging them verbally with questions and observations. A traditional nursery school may also have a strong resemblance to a Direct Instruction program. I visited a twenty-year-old program run in a church by a grandmotherly woman who had the children copying her drawings of local birds—a classic example of teacher-directed activity. And at a Montessori school, where I expected to find emphasis on sensory exploration initiated by the child under a teacher's guidance (similar to the High/Scope approach), there was one classroom wall decorated with the children's identical drawings of the solar system—also direct instruction.

Far more important than the name or philosophy a preschool claims to endorse, according to most child-care experts, is a caring, qualified staff and a setting in which your child will feel comfortable. "I think most good teachers and directors take a little of this and a little of that from different approaches—whatever works," one nursery-school teacher told me. When it comes to preschools, a label is no guarantee that a program is high in quality or even that it truly follows a particular educational philosophy.

Let's take Montessori schools as an example.

Read Maria Montessori's writings on the education of young children in her Case dei Bambini, or Children's Houses, for the Roman poor after the turn of the century, and you cannot help being struck by a number of highly admirable features:

- Her respect for the child's natural ability and desire to learn. ("Humanity shows itself in all its intellectual splendour during this tender age as the sun shows itself at the dawn, and the flower in the first unfolding of the petals; and we must *respect* religiously, reverently, these first indications of individuality," she writes in *The Montessori Method.*)

- Her ability to view the world from a child's perspective, beginning with her insistence that her classrooms be equipped with child-size furniture.

- Her understanding that preschoolers learn through sensory manipulation (which is why her "didactic materials" included three-dimensional alphabet letters made of sandpaper, long before the magnetic refrigerator variety came on the scene).

■ Her willingness to help children take responsibility for care of themselves and their environment (by learning to serve meals with child-size utensils and plates, and by learning to fasten their clothes and brush their teeth, for example).

Look at the American Montessori Society pamphlet *Basic Characteristics of a Montessori Program for 3 to 6 Year Old Children* and you are informed that the Montessori child is a "responsible group member," that children learn through "intrinsic motivation" (for the sake of learning, rather than to please the teacher), and that there is a "natural social environment" in the classroom. Sounds good, right? Yet Montessori teachers are sometimes criticized for interpreting "intrinsic motivation" as an excuse to remain distant from the children and offer no encouragement or praise. And as for group responsibility and the social environment, Montessori programs are often criticized for placing so much emphasis on each child's right to "work" that social interaction falls by the wayside. (Here children are said to work, not play, in accord with Montessori's famous saying, "Play is a child's work.")

In a Montessori classroom children from three to six are grouped together, so that the older ones teach the younger ones. They have the freedom to move around and decide what they want to "work" on at a particular time, rather than being constricted by organized group activities. "Didactic materials" are laid out in neat order on shelves easily accessible to children. The teacher's role is that of a resource person who decides when the child is ready to move from simple to more complex exercises using the learning materials. As one expert explains it, in Maria Montessori's classrooms, "the important relationship was not between child and teacher but between child and materials." Pretend play and creative expression take a backseat to sensory manipulation and lessons designed to prepare the child for reading, writing, and math as well as "practical life." Instead of toy vehicles and building blocks, there are

■ clothing frames with buttons, hooks, snaps, and ties to help children learn to dress themselves. There are also

■ sequentially ordered "sensory" materials, such as cylinder blocks which the child learns to nest according to diameter. These materials are "self-correcting," or designed to prevent the child from making errors.

While Montessori's hands-on approach to learning was a great step forward in her time, when children were expected to be seen and not heard, today many early-childhood educators object that it is unnecessarily rigid. "They take beautiful open-ended materials," comments Margaret Bloodgood of the City and Country School, "and say, 'You *have* to use them this way.' "

Others complain that children are deprived of the opportunity for creative art experiences, that fantasy and imagination are discouraged, and that the *real* rationale behind Montessori is to teach early academics. One of Montessori's basic precepts—the one that has made her the darling of parents caught in the super-baby syndrome, no doubt—is that the preschool child has an "absorbent mind" ideally suited to learn to recognize and write the letters of the alphabet. "Montessori, like all other chic, popular programs, will attract certain parents because they think that they'll get a leg up," admits Bretta Weiss, national director of the American Montessori Society. "They think it will get their children into the best schools, and eventually into Harvard at fifteen. It's a distortion and it's a lack of understanding of Montessori's aims." Nonetheless, while other nursery-school kids are playing with fire trucks and finger paints, Montessori children are tracing sandpaper letters. And the AMS pamphlet on Montessori kindergarten notes with obvious satisfaction that "the goals of a Montessori classroom seem to be more closely related to those of a traditional first-grade class than those of a traditional kindergarten."

One can practically see parents drooling over *that* one. But should they be? "The question is, if this is the time that they're 'absorbing,' what do you care most about having them absorb?" asks Margaret Bloodgood. "Do you want them to learn how to deal with other people? Do you want them to learn what their world is and how to express themselves about it? Or do you want them to learn the alphabet? If this is their 'prime time,' then it seems to me that one should expose them to things that are *really* essential—how the world works, how they cope, who they are."

How does Bretta Weiss reply to this criticism? "All I can say in terms of the early academics is that the charge is true that they're present in the classroom," she replies. "The charge is not true that a child is in any way coerced, or that there's any kind of thrust to make [early academic study] the center of his time in that school."

Unfortunately, that depends which Montessori school you're talking about. I visited one where a five-year-old boy was being scolded for getting his multiplication table wrong.

"There's tremendous variation from one school to another," says Weiss. "But if a parent sends a child to Montessori in order to learn to read and write at the age of three, then that child is under such a terrible pressure and strain that he's probably not going to do well. There's no reason whatsoever to believe that just by entering a Montessori class a child is suddenly going to be reading the *Times* by the age of five."

As practiced in real-life classrooms, Montessori methods vary considerably from the Casa dei Bambini prototype—and from one another, too. Today, the teacher's role is usually more active than that of the observer Montessori envisioned. "Montessori materials alone certainly do not direct all the activity of the child," admits Bretta Weiss. "That's impossible. They're good learning materials, but you have to have more than that—and the child will find more than that." A good Montessori classroom, she says, includes art supplies, Lego bricks, and even (dare we say the word?) toys.

So how do you know whether you're looking at a good Montessori school? By checking it out as thoroughly as you'd check out any other school *without* a label.

Healthy Ways to Help

Before you even visit a prospective nursery school for your child, it's worthwhile doing some homework: by sitting down and giving some thought to your *goals* in sending him or her to preschool, you're in a much better position to evaluate the programs you see (and the sales pitches you may hear). Keep in mind that while few early-childhood specialists believe that drills and worksheets on the alphabet and numbers belong in a nursery-school setting, that doesn't mean your child shouldn't be learning. But the kind of learning that takes place in a good nursery school is different, and in many ways far more difficult to measure.

The program should foster every aspect of a young child's development—physical, emotional, social, and cognitive—and offer plenty of opportunity for her to explore her environment under the guidance of a trained, sensitive teacher. "Our goal is to encourage children's natural desire to learn things, and not to smother that impulse," says Margaret Bloodgood. "In nursery school children can begin to learn about the learning process. They can begin to express their feelings and express their perceptions of how different parts of their world relate to each other."

Nursery school is a time when many early-childhood experts believe your child is developing not only knowledge and skills but *dispositions,* or habits of thinking that will stay with her all her life. She is not only learning her colors and numerals, how to put on her snowpants and hold a pencil, but developing her curiosity about the world around her, her creativity, and her persistence at problem-solving. For this reason, she will benefit most from a program that encourages *active* learning and hands-on exploration, rather than merely teaching kids to parrot abstract facts and recognize two-dimensional symbols.

Many nursery schools publish glossy brochures and invite parents of prospective students to open houses where teachers talk about the program. These can be good ways to hear some noble sentiments about preschool education, and you may even get some insight into the director's philosophy. But they are no substitute for an unhurried visit to the classroom on a regular school day, where you can see the kids and teachers in action. One university-affiliated preschool sent me a slick brochure filled with caring prose about children's curiosity, friendships, and creativity, accompanied by captivating photos of three-year-olds busy at sand tables and story corners. When I viewed the class through a two-way mirror, I was shocked to see the *teacher* throwing a temper tantrum at her small charges, shouting, "You are all rude children!" as they ran wild around the tables and easels.

Make an appointment in advance so that you can also use the opportunity to ask the director a few questions. Then consider these points:

Five Steps to Finding a Good Preschool for Your Child

1. *The Staff* The nuts and bolts: You have a right to know about the background, training, and experience of the school's director and teachers. Ask about the adult-to-child ratio (the NAEYC recommends no more than twenty four-year-olds to two adults), and how many of the teachers and aides have training in early-childhood education. Ask how long most members of the staff have been there. (If teachers quit mid-year, the disruption can be highly traumatic for a class of young children.) If the school is a cooperative, are parents expected to teach? If so, how often, and what guidelines are they given by the staff?

Next, the teaching style; but first, let's hear from the NAEYC's *Good Teaching Practices for 4- and 5-Year-Olds.* This position statement declares emphatically that "the correct way to teach young children is not to lecture or verbally instruct them. Teachers of young children are more like guides or facilitators . . . They prepare the environment so that it provides stimulating, challenging materials and activities for children. Then, teachers closely observe to see what children understand and pose additional challenges to push their thinking further."

Sounds like a hard thing to check on, doesn't it? Happily, there are a number of ways to spot a teacher who takes this active but not overbearing approach. It's a good sign, for example, if she bends or squats down to talk with the kids at their level. Watch whether she listens attentively to what they have to say. Does she answer their questions thoughtfully, with more than a yes or a no? Does she seem affectionate, understanding that young children respond to touch? Does she only comment on children's behavior when it is negative, or does she offer praise as well, such as, "You did a good job putting away the blocks"? Does she seem to enjoy the children? How does she handle the less glorious aspects of teaching young children—say, the child who needs his shoes tied, or has an "accident" on the floor?

No matter how good the teacher, expect to see a squabble or two among the children during your visit. "It's wonderful if you can come in and there's a little dispute going on," comments Margaret Bloodgood. "That tells you much more than if everybody's having a wonderful time: if Johnny just hit Patty on the head with his blocks, see how the teacher handles that." Does she talk to Johnny clearly? Does she remove him from the situation immediately? Is she able to contain the problem and prevent it from disrupting the rest of the class?

Keep in mind that it's important not to limit your viewing to the teacher your child would have if she were to enroll. Obviously, there may be a change in staff from one year to the next, and watching several teachers in action is a good way to get a sense of the school as a whole.

2. *The Children* Are they attentive when the teacher speaks? Are they absorbed in their individual activities? Are some playing together—perhaps building a collective block creation or cooking dinner in the toy kitchen? Are they talking among themselves? Do they approach the teacher with questions and creations to show her?

Do the children appear to understand the routine and the rules? Are they busy during free play? Do they cooperate during "circle," or group, time? Do they pay attention as a story is being read?

Perhaps most important, do the children appear to be initiating their own learning activities, deciding what to do and how to do it? The teacher should create a framework—by organizing materials, bringing out different things each day, and structuring the session into various segments (free play, storytime, and so on)—but should allow the children the opportunity to learn to make choices.

3. *The Environment* Young children feel secure in a nursery-school environment that is as *homey and comfortable* as possible. There should be carpeted areas where they can sit, child-size tables and chairs, and cubbies or bins (individually labeled with each child's name and photograph) for clothing and items brought from home. The materials available should be rich and varied, accessible to the children, and well organized: Look for a dress-up area, a kitchen, a block area, easels and art supplies, a sand or water table, a story corner with books displayed so that the children can see the covers, and an outdoor area with safe climbing and play equipment (climbing frames, trikes, and so on).

Do you see a balance between *structured* activities, such as puzzles and peg boards, and *open-ended* ones (clay, paint, blocks, and water)? Is there evidence that the children *cook,* listen to and make *music,* explore *nature,* and care for *plants* or *animals?*

Is *printed material* used in the classroom? Toy bins should be labeled, and on the wall you should expect to see written materials, such as a calendar, charts listing the day's helpers or class birthdays, or stories dictated by the children. Are writing tools and paper available for the children to produce written expression?

Don't be dazzled by the sight of a *computer.* Check to see whether it is a major brand and of relatively recent vintage—otherwise there may be little or no preschool software available for it. "There are a lot of dinosaurs out there that have been donated to preschools by individuals or companies looking for a tax write-off," says Charles Hohmann, Ph.D., an expert on children and computers with the High/Scope Educational Research Foundation. Ask what computer experience the teachers have had. Here practice counts more than time spent in courses hearing instructors explain how computers work. "What they really need is hands-on experience using early-childhood software," says Dr. Hohmann. This software should not be limited to drills on the ABCs and numbers, but should offer opportunities for simple games and computer graphics or "paint" programs. Finally, the computer should be set up in the classroom as a learning center—just like the kitchen or block area—and children should be able to use it, independently or in small groups, at will.

4. *The School's Attitude Toward Parents* Does the school have a planned-separation policy, allowing parents to be present for a few sessions at the start of the year before the child feels comfortable on her own? Can parents view classes whenever they wish? Are parent-teacher conferences scheduled as part of the program? Are teachers available for informal talks when no conference is scheduled? Does the school offer activities for parents, such as a support group or lectures on child-rearing issues? Does the teacher seem interested in knowing about the child's home life—siblings, baby-sitters, and so on?

5. *Your Own "Gut Reaction"* Once you've considered all the details, ask yourself whether the school feels like a happy place, one where your child would feel comfortable. Sometimes your reaction may not seem logical, but it's hard to go wrong by following your instincts. "I nearly put my child in a nursery school that feeds into some of the fanciest private schools in our area," one mother told me. "Then a ten-year-old neighbor girl asked me, 'You're sending Ruthie to ——, aren't you? I really loved it when I went there.' I decided to go with that school, which I'd been impressed by anyway, and after a year there I must say, Ruthie couldn't be happier."

On the other hand, don't ignore negative feelings about a nursery school even if everybody else thinks it's a little Harvard. "I think parents should really pay attention when they go to a school and say, 'I don't like it, but I don't know why,'" says Margaret Bloodgood. "They shouldn't just say, 'Oh, it has a wonderful reputation, and the teacher's so nice, and all the children go to Ivy League schools.' There's probably a very good reason for them not to like it."

Keep in mind that your feelings may reflect the fact that you understand your child better than anyone else. Only you can know when a school may be perfectly good but simply not the right place for your child at that particular stage. In choosing my son's first nursery school, for example, I eliminated one school (which happened to be our local Montessori) on the grounds that the classroom's well-organized shelves contained not a single toy truck. At two and one-half, he considered trucks the center of the universe, and I could not see him adjusting successfully to school without a few to play with. Bretta Weiss, national director of the American Montessori Society, agrees with this approach. "Mentally put your child into the environment and think about how he would feel," she suggests. "Try to see him operating there, see him sitting there, and look around to see what's available for him and what you think he would like."

In the long run, your child can learn two important lessons from her time in nursery school. She can begin to learn all that is involved in getting along with others—sharing, cooperating, making friends, waiting her turn, listening, explaining, and so on. And she can get the idea that active learning is fun—that school is a place where she can experiment with different materials and discover exciting new worlds to explore. Lessons such as these can't be pinned down on worksheets or through drills, but it's hard to imagine more valuable preparation for her school days or, later on, for life in the world of grown-ups.

Is the "Sesame Street" Generation Really Smarter?

Two-year-old: "One, two, three, four, five, six, seven, eight, nine, TEN!"

Mother (beaming): "He learned that from 'Sesame Street'!"

Two-year-old: "Me want cookie! Me cookie!"

Mother (wincing): "He learned that from 'Sesame Street.' "

ASK MOST PARENTS what they think about children's television and they shrug and thank God (and the networks) that it's on while they're fixing dinner. "Sesame Street" is different. There are those who strap their ten-month-olds into high chairs aimed at "Sesame Street" in the firm belief that the show is indispensable to brain development. Somehow our generation of parents has bought into the idea that tuning in daily to Big Bird and the gang is something today's superbaby *ought* to do. Parents eager to produce "advanced" progeny are parking their unsuspecting kids in front of the set as soon as they learn to sit up. If Junior watches twice a day, why worry? This is educational television—the more the better. Add in a few videotaped segments (homemade or those marketed by Golden Books) and the sky's the limit. You get some peace and quiet; your child effortlessly learns to read and count. You can fan the fires of your child's enthusiasm by buying him a few "Sesame Street" dolls, a training cup, a jack-in-the-box, or a precomputer—all featuring his favorite Muppet characters.

Sound too good to be true? Well, many critics believe that it is. Scroogelike though it may be to suggest that Kermit and company might not be a young child's best teachers, these curmudgeons have dared to point out that "Sesame Street," for all its good points, needs to be seen in perspective. In the wasteland of children's television, "Sesame Street" is clearly one of the least offensive shows on the air. Nonetheless, it is still television, and therefore of limited value as a learning tool. In fact, many child-development specialists maintain that television is essentially *incompatible with the young child's natural approach to learning.* Ironically, many of the most frequent criticisms of "Sesame Street" are directed at the show's attempts to overcome the medium's limitations, as we shall see.

At first blush, questioning the educational value of "educational television" makes as much sense as denouncing disposable diapers. "No matter what 'Sesame Street' does that isn't perfect, it's nowhere near as bad as 'My Little Pony' and 'Care Bears' and 'Transformers' and 'G.I. Joe' and stuff that's designed to pitch a product to kids," says Peggy Charren, president of the watchdog group Action for Children's Television (ACT), based in Cambridge, Massachusetts. "When that's the kind of stuff that's available, and children are watching it in droves, worrying about 'Sesame Street' seems to me rather nonproductive."

Few would deny that the show is an oasis of nonviolence and noble intentions in the desert of what ACT calls "chase-and-bop" shows and "program-length commercials" that glut the airwaves.

The *subject matter* of "Sesame Street"—the brief "field trips" to farms and factories, the sequences on cooperation and sharing, the focus on human diversity—stands in sharp contrast to the warring tribes at other points on the dial. But with the average preschooler watching no less than *four and one-half hours of television per day,* according to ACT, whether or not "Sesame Street" does more for a child's development than (dare we suggest it?) *turning off the set* and offering him an opportunity to learn from his environment may be a highly productive question to ask. Parents who encourage their kids to watch videotapes of the show for hours on end, or who tune it in via cable TV anywhere from two to four times a day, need to hear exactly what "Sesame Street" can teach a child—and what it can't.

For the fact is, many experts are far from convinced that the subject matter of "Sesame Street" makes up for the show's very real drawbacks for the young child. They emphasize that the *medium* is still television, with all its sterility for the pint-size pioneer who needs to learn through firsthand sensory exploration—not a flat screen. Such critics believe strongly that preschool learning comes about through the child's self-driven attempts to explore his *three-dimensional* environment, from the kitchen faucet to his toy xylophone—not lounging in front of a TV set, no matter which channel it's tuned to. When you're dazzled by the show's ability to teach numbers and letters, it's easy to ignore this fact and come to revere "Sesame Street" as an electronic miracle-worker. Instead of worrying that your child may be watching too much TV, you assume it's okay because after all, aren't you scrupulously keeping him away from commercial programming? As freelance writer Jody Gaylin has written in a recent autobiographical article "TV Cold Turkey," published in *Parents,* "My oldest, as a toddler, was barely interested in the little television he saw and I was pretty picky about what that was—'Sesame Street,' maybe a little 'Mister Rogers' Neighborhood' but *no* commercial stations. . . . But somehow the amount of TV he watched began to creep up on us. . . . With cable, "Sesame Street" is available several times a day, and the hours of watching increased." Although Gaylin had made it a point to veto commercial TV, she had easily let her child drift into hours of watching the "educational" variety.

Also, many child-development experts believe that "Sesame Street," because of its emphasis on counting and the alphabet, bolsters an unfortunate tendency among today's parents to believe that numbers and letters are the most important lessons a preschooler needs to learn. "It may be that it's a symptom of some underlying anxiety parents have about how to insure their kids' future," comments Irving Segal of the Educational Testing Service in Princeton, New Jersey, who has spoken out repeatedly in the media against the superbaby syndrome. "Most parents are trying to do the right thing; I'm only going to fault them for not trying to understand development. My objection to 'Sesame Street' is that *anything* that induces and seduces the kid into inactivity is a danger because good thinking comes from *action*. . . . What we want kids to be is active learners." In other words, sitting and passively watching is not learning.

Unfortunately, parents remain unaware of what kids are *failing* to learn by watching the show. Most of the highly publicized research on children's television has rightly focused on the effects of violence and commercials on young children, rather than on the ineffectiveness of TV teaching. Thus the harm done by television through displacing more valuable learning activities remains largely obscured.

Besides, since most parents watch a great deal of television themselves, and since there's no denying that the set can be a very convenient baby-sitter, it's not too surprising that they assume young children should be watching television, especially if it's a show that promises as much as "Sesame Street." But even if you don't agree that television is a "plug-in drug," as education writer Marie Winn calls it, it's certainly no plug-in professor, either. Let's see why not.

Counting Is Such Fun!

Perhaps the best-known critic of "Sesame Street" has been the communications theorist Neil Postman. In his 1985 book *Amusing Ourselves to Death,* Postman calls the show the answer to a guilty parent's prayer: " 'Sesame Street' appeared to justify allowing a four- or five-year-old to sit transfixed in front of a television screen for unnatural periods of time. Parents were eager to hope that television could teach their children something other than which breakfast cereal has the most crackle . . ."

Building on Marshall McLuhan's now-clichéd aphorism "The medium is the message," Postman points out that television by its very nature is the antithesis of true education. First of all, it is a *visual* medium. Unlike fairy tales, nursery rhymes, and storybooks, whose essence is language, television is a series of images. It may present elements of reading, such as the alphabet, but it offers no opportunity to use them, no chance to experience how they work. A child cannot truly interact with or explore an object in the world of television; he can't touch it, shake it, or turn it upside down. He can't hold the apples being flashed on the screen in his hand and count them.

Equally important, it is a *passive* medium. No matter how sympathetic or appealing a performer on the screen may be, he can't answer a child's questions. "It's not a question of what kids *are* learning—it's what they're *not* doing while they're watching. Life is more than sitting in front of a box with pictures, no matter how delightful and meaningful the pictures can be," says ACT's Peggy Charren. "You don't talk when you're watching television. You don't talk back. You don't do for yourself, you don't make things. You don't even kick stones."

In 1984, the American Academy of Pediatrics issued a policy statement entitled *Children, Adolescents, and Television,* noting that "learning from television is passive rather than active, and detracts from time spent reading or using active learning skills." Even little kids know this. Try to get your child to leave for nursery school, sit down to lunch, or go to bed after a long sojourn in front of the tube, and what's his protest? "But I didn't have time to *play!"*

Because it is two-dimensional, even TV at best can never give a child a real understanding of anything. It can only *demonstrate* concepts. This is where "Sesame Street" has had its biggest success—and encountered its strongest criticism. Unlike the dull productions seen on educational television when *we* were kids, "Sesame Street" was designed to make learning from TV fun. When the show was first conceived by Children's Television Workshop in 1968, its original purpose was to use television to teach *disadvantaged* young children. As a 1971 ETS study pointed out, "Sesame Street" "was not developed as a substitute for an educationally excellent nursery school. . . . Rather it was meant as an ingredient for the educational diet of the millions of three-through five-year-old children who do not have the opportunity of going to preschool." This target audience was assumed to be deprived of a multitude of enriching daily experiences, from conversations to toys to library and museum visits. "We still take a special interest in the disadvantaged child," says Valeria Lovelace, Ph.D., director of research for "Sesame Street." "The idea is, if we can target [the program] for the child who has nothing in the home except that television set, making it very concrete and understandable to children who may not have a mother there to explain, or may not have a book to hook into, then there are all sorts of benefits . . ."

To this end, CTW drew up a "curriculum" that would spell out those benefits as precisely as possible. "Now the curriculum has grown to over two hundred goals," says Dr. Lovelace. "We try to teach children about their body parts. We try to teach children about planning and imagining. We try to teach children about letters and numbers and a variety of mathematical concepts." (The Statement of Instructional Goals for the 1987–1988 season, for example, includes everything from storybook reading to computers to toothbrushing.)

By playing with you, taking the occasional weekend outing to the zoo, and playing with blocks, *your* child will delight in learning where his nose is, or what a zebra looks like, or that two halves make a whole. The child for whom "Sesame Street" was developed lacks those opportunities. What Children's Television Workshop has done is *accept* the fact that the two-dimensional world of television cannot offer the child the satisfaction of the self-motivated, hands-on learning he might enjoy in a more responsive home environment, and has come up with a bag of video tricks to provide a substitute brand of excitement. Animated numbers and letters fly around the screen, puppets play rhyming games, Bert and Ernie talk about sharing.

When the show was being developed, researchers watched children viewing it to determine which segments best held their attention. They gave the thumbs-up sign to such features as

- simple, clear language in short speeches

- rhythm and rhyme

- lively music

- children's voices

- peculiar voices

- changes in sound and sound effects

- clear plot with fairly predictable outcome.

What got the thumbs-down? Among other things, song-and-dance numbers, men's voices, and live animals. Perish the thought that with time and exposure a child might cultivate a taste for one of these elements—didn't kids once love Captain Kangaroo? In the harsh world of today's children's TV, if something doesn't grab them from the word go, it's gone. Unfortunately, say many critics, when you try to direct a preschooler's learning from outside while he sits passively watching, rather than encourage his own exploration, you cause his attention to flag. And so you need to resort to fun and games, packaged in fast-forward for maximum viewer appeal and eliminating anything that can't be swallowed as quickly as an M&M. That's why Neil Postman characterizes watching "Sesame Street" as "being *taught* by a series of commercials." And why the British Broadcasting Company (according to a recent report in the *New York Times*) refused to air the show on the grounds that, with its quick succession of short takes, it was "too hectic."

How does Children's Television Workshop respond to criticism that the show is so fast-paced as to be hyperstimulating to a young child? "Actually, it's varied," says Valeria Lovelace. "On the average, our segments are about a minute and a half long. And in many [segments of] the 'Street,' we stay there for about two and a half minutes, three minutes, sometimes four." These are eternities in televisionland, no doubt, but a far cry from the hours a preschooler can spend digging away in a sandbox or building a block tower when offered the opportunity.

Furthermore, because this brand of learning emanates not from the child but from an electronic box, the child's enthusiasm for the lessons on the screen has to be pumped up through constant cheerleading. "Counting is such fun!" exclaims the Count. Actually, as most taxpayers know, counting isn't particularly fun. We count—just as we read and write—*as a means to an end.* We want to balance a checkbook, get the sports scores, or add up our day's caloric consumption. In the real world, children are motivated to learn this way, too: the child may enjoy reciting the numbers, but he counts to five *with understanding* when he wants to make sure, for example, that he gets just as many raisin-oatmeal cookies as his big sister. Unlike the "Sesame Street" viewer, who merely parrots the names of the numbers he hears on a voice-over, *this* child can *feel* how many cookies he has in his hot little hand. When he shouts triumphantly, "That's *my* cookie because she already has *three!*" you can be confident that he's developed a genuine concept of number. And his attention will be riveted to the activity of cookie-counting until he's satisfied that he's got his fair share out of the cookie jar—even if it takes a whole lot longer than the typical ninety-second TV segment.

Likewise, the child who learns his letters through the experience of being read to is gaining much more than if he were rattling off the ABCs. In the process, he learns a great deal about the contents of books. As we have seen, he becomes familiar with the conventions of fiction. Hearing one story after another in its entirety, he gets the sense that a plot has a beginning, middle, and end. He comes to know that characters can grow and change with experience and the passage of time. He understands that conflicts can develop between characters, and witnesses their resolution, usually after a few false starts. These are complex ideas that require *time.* They can't be delivered in the fleeting video sequences kids glimpse on "Sesame Street" or any other television show. From nonfiction books, the child discovers that a reader has the power to find answers to his questions on virtually any subject that takes his fancy. In contrast to the TV viewer, whose visits to a peanut-butter factory or balloon race are dependent on the day's program schedule, a reader can actively *choose* what he wants to learn more about. But if the TV set is blaring all day long and he's mesmerized in front of it, when will he engage in these active learning experiences?

Unlike flashy graphics and razzle-dazzle, these are the lessons that most child-development experts believe will propel a child through a lifetime of learning. Many educators, like Neil Postman, have voiced concern that "Sesame Street" minimizes the *inherent satisfaction* learning provides, and instead sells preschoolers on the idea that learning is nothing *but* fun. As Postman puts it in *Amusing Ourselves to Death,* the message is that learning is a form of entertainment, "or, more precisely, that anything worth learning can take the form of an entertainment, and ought to. And they will not rebel if their English teacher asks them to learn the eight parts of speech through the medium of rock music. Or if their social studies teacher sings to them the facts about the

War of 1812. Or if their physics comes to them on cookies and T-shirts."

Many early-childhood educators have voiced concern that kids weaned on "Sesame Street," though better versed in the ABCs than past generations, seem to have trouble believing traditional school learning *is* fun, once they've made the switch from Kermit to kindergarten and first grade. When they make the break from leaping letters and numbers to old-fashioned books, it can be rough going, because TV lessons are *only a small part of what it takes to prepare a child for school.* Motivation to learn, imagination, and problem-solving skills are the real prerequisites for academic success, and a child can only develop them through active exploration of the environment.

That's why, when you hear reports that regular "Sesame Street" viewers have racked up impressive scores on standardized tests, it pays to take a closer look. From 1969 through 1971 the Educational Testing Service studied two thousand preschoolers from all over the country to find out what they were learning from the show. Its researchers found that the show *was* effective in teaching "some basic facts and skills," such as letters and numbers, to children aged three to six. But that doesn't tell you a whole lot about what it does for a child's intelligence, curiosity, enthusiasm for learning, or even reading readiness in its broadest sense.

"In the sense of reading at a decoding level, it may well be that 'Sesame Street' has contributed to kids' attention to the letters of the alphabet. Kindergarten teachers will say that kids now come to kindergarten knowing that class of information, where twenty years ago they didn't. I'm sure TV is part of that," says Edward Chittendon, a senior research psychologist at ETS, who has done extensive research into the way children learn to read. "Are they ready to read? Well, they're ready to deal with *print,* perhaps, in the sense of decoding. But there's a distinction between learning to read and *becoming a reader.* The same kindergarten teachers will say that children seem less familiar with some of the literature—stories and fairy tales. . . . Kindergarten teachers have been telling me in recent years that it's harder to get kids to listen to that than it used to be."

Even "Sesame Street" 's director of research is careful to point out that the show is not designed to create superbabies. "No one kind of learning experience can create those," states Valeria Lovelace. Dr. Lovelace is currently doing research exploring the long-term results of viewing the program. "I'm working with adults now who grew up watching 'Sesame Street.' I think some of them are bright individuals, and I think some of them are not so bright," she admits. "So I can't say that that sheds any light on 'Sesame Street' per se. It's *one factor* in the socialization of these kids." Stay tuned: Dr. Lovelace expects the results of her study to be available in late 1988.

Where Did the Bulldozer Go, Mommy?

Part of the problem, say many experts, is that children who grow up with lots of television don't learn to pay attention deliberately. Instead, the set attracts them like a magnet. Just as adults are irresistibly drawn to commercials for squeezable toilet paper and antiperspirant—topics that would never make the best-seller list as *books*—kids watch the TV screen because they *can't help watching it.* There's something happening every minute. And "Sesame Street" is no exception. After all, that's exactly the effect it was designed to create.

Research has shown that kids don't even have to pay much attention to the TV in order to learn their numbers and letters from "Sesame Street." During the late 1970s and early 1980s, a group of researchers at the University of Massachusetts studied preschoolers watching "Sesame Street" under a variety of conditions. They compared how much of the program the children remembered and understood while watching in a room containing a variety of toys with how much they remembered in a room with no toys at all. Surprisingly, they found that although the preschoolers looked at the screen significantly more when they had no toys to play with, they recalled and understood *equal amounts* of material under both conditions. As the researchers explained, when children look away from the television they listen for clues that tell them to look back (not unlike the way adults know it's time to return from the refrigerator once they hear a commercial is over). Even very young viewers quickly learn to distinguish the sounds (music, the appearance of new characters, and so on) that mean something new is being presented.

As a result, the kids learn the ABCs just as you might find yourself humming the jingle from a hot-dog commercial. What concerns educators, though, is that these pint-size viewers have *not* been prepared at all to engage in the kind of thinking they will need to cope with learning later on in school—or even to read a book. They are learning through repetition, also known as brainwashing. Because there is so much action on the television screen, a child has no time to stop and reflect on what he has seen, no time to try and make sense of it, or to truly internalize it. The rapid-fire images are intended to be consumed as quickly as salted French fries, not analyzed, and the child becomes accustomed to receiving information without thinking about it much. As the psychologists Jerome and Dorothy Singer of the Yale University Family Television Research and Consultation Center have suggested, "It may be that attracting attention to the screen in the way it does, 'Sesame Street' may be maximizing an unreflective viewing stance . . ."

Margaret Bloodgood agrees. "We don't care for 'Sesame Street' because it doesn't allow the child to use his own mind. It doesn't allow the children to think things through and work things out *for themselves,*" she says. "Everything just darts from here to there, and it doesn't make any sense. It's a fast-paced, get-what-you-want-now, impatient, never-stop-to-smell-anything approach."

For many young children this madcap pace can even be confusing. The very first time my son watched "Sesame Street"—at around eighteen months of age—he wound up furious at the television set. He'd started out in a burst of enthusiasm when a short film clip on building construction had come on. "Look, a bulldozer!" he'd squealed in delight. But in a flash the film clip was over, the bulldozer vanished, and Bert and Ernie had launched into a typical bickering session. Matthew stared at the screen in puzzled dismay: "Where did bulldozer go?" he asked. I tried to explain that the bulldozer part of the program was over, that we were watching something else fun right now, but there was no comforting him. He posted himself in front of the set like a sentry, alert for any reappearance by the missing bulldozer. When it failed to materialize, Matthew seemed to decide that television wasn't much fun at all.

Matthew's "problem" was his lack of familiarity with the conventions of television. When you really think about it, that a toddler or young preschooler ends up baffled by all these goings-on isn't too surprising. After all, TV plays fast and loose with time, logic, and space—people arrive at destinations without spending any time getting there, they sing with accompaniment and you can't for the life of you see a piano, and multiton vehicles appear and disappear at the drop of a hat. Most young children are barely coming to grips with these concepts in real life. As Jerome and Dorothy Singer put it in one of their scholarly articles, "Extremely rapidly paced material that presents much novelty along with higher levels of sound, fast movement, intercutting, etc., may generate surprise and indeed confusion in a viewer whose anticipatory strategies or well-established schemata are not yet prepared for coping with this material." According to a 1976 study by the Singers, even the gentle, patient Mister Rogers, who carefully explains every detail of what he is doing and takes almost as long as a three-year-old to put on his sneakers, may not be fully understood by three- and four-year-olds. Admittedly, books such as *Peter Rabbit* and *Babar* are often bewildering to the preschool mind, but there is a parent or care-giver reading the story who can interpret and answer questions. When the TV functions as a baby-sitter, the child has no adult to help sort out the world on the screen, and it's often very different from the one in which he lives.

Small wonder that NBC found it necessary to air brief announcements between Saturday morning programs, warning children not to try to fly or run through brick walls. Apparently not all viewers had reached the level of cognitive development or life experience to know they can't really perform these feats!

Some of the TV tricks on "Sesame Street," in particular, can be puzzling to a child left to watch alone. For example:

- Aspects of the format that are designed to be a take-off on commercials (" 'Sesame Street' has been brought to you by the letter *J* ") can be confusing to a young child who has never watched commercial television and doesn't get the joke. (And even when the parent is there to explain it, why would we and PBS want to encourage the belief that commercials—even make-believe ones—are an essential and even desirable part of TV?)

- The use of frequent intercutting and short clips (again, in imitation of commercials) is very different from the real world, where objects are usually seen in context and action has continuity through time. One mother told me that her son watched a "Sesame Street" video on which a school bus, labeled *B-U-S,* darted across the screen and back. "Where was the bus going, Mommy?" asked her three-and-a-half-year-old. "Where were the people going on the bus?" To build on this preschooler's curiosity and imagination, the mother might have turned off the set and encouraged him to speculate on the bus's destination. The alternative is to let the child resign himself to the fact that on TV things just seem to happen without rhyme, reason, or context, and why bother trying to make sense of it?

- The use of ironic humor—presumably to keep parents amused enough to tune in—has been found to be especially puzzling to children *up to fourth grade,* according to Dolf Zillman, a psychologist at Indiana University and author of *Handbook of Humor Research* (1983). Because they do not yet have the basic knowledge that allows them to understand what is true and what is a distortion, they can't appreciate the humor of, say, "Sesame Street" 's depiction of seat belts on an airplane: when the plane turns upside down, the seat-belted characters hang from the cockpit as if the belts were rubber. Obviously, public TV deserves to be applauded for staying away from the violence and scary scenes in commercial programming that can overwhelm a child; but unfortunately, flying alphabets and rubber seat belts can also be overwhelming in their own way. And what happens when a child is overwhelmed by the TV set? Instead of using learning as an active process that rewards his natural urge to understand his world, he discovers that confusing images will soon disappear from the screen to be replaced by others that are less puzzling, so there's no point in working at it.

The highly respected pediatrician and author T. Berry Brazelton, M.D., writing in *The ACT Guide to Children's Television* (1979), compares a child's reaction to TV with a newborn's response to overstimulation. Citing research he did to explore how newborns responded when a bright operating-room light was turned on two feet away from their heads, Brazelton observes that a tiny infant "has a marvelous mechanism, a shutdown device, for dealing with disturbing stimuli: he can tune them out and go into a sleeplike state." The thumbsucking toddler or preschooler who likes to "veg out" in front of the tube is doing much the same thing. "For just like the operating-room light, television creates an environment that assaults and overwhelms the child," writes Brazelton. "He can respond to it only by bringing into play his shutdown mechanism and thus becomes more passive." Dr. Brazelton concludes by recommending that children under the age of five or six spend no more than *one hour a day* in front of the set.

Healthy Ways to Help

Does all this mean you shouldn't let your preschooler watch "Sesame Street"? Admittedly, that's impractical in most households, where preschoolers are watching all kinds of programs for as much as three to four hours a day. As Jerome and Dorothy Singer state flatly in *Make Believe: Games and Activities to Foster Imaginative Play in Young Children* (1985), "It is our personal belief that it would be better for children's development if they saw no TV at all until they were of school age, with well-established habits of reading. Parents . . . would have no difficulty in providing them with many imaginative resources without TV. . . . We recognize that 99 percent of the parents will have no such inclination. Therefore, it makes sense to accept television and try to find out how to make the best use of this extremely powerful medium."

Keep in mind that the research does show that television's capacity to teach preschoolers is extremely limited without caring participation by you, the parent. It's important to *monitor* your particular child's reactions, *limit* his viewing, and try to *integrate* the material he sees on television with his everyday life. Alas, this approach makes it hard to use television as an electronic baby-sitter. On the bright side, however, spending less time in front of the TV set—and getting more out of it—may help your child discover a new world of fantasy and imagination inside himself that will keep him happily occupied for longer than you ever thought possible. As Bruno Bettelheim observes in his book *A Good-Enough Parent*, "A lack of sufficient leisure to develop a rich inner life is a large part of the reason why a child will pressure his parents to entertain him or will turn on the television set. . . . In a vicious circle, the lack of a chance to spend much of his energies on his inner life causes the child to turn to readily available stimuli for filling an inner void, and these stimuli then constitute another obstacle to the child's development of his inner life."

Here are five steps designed to make the most of television for your preschooler—and still leave him plenty of opportunity to develop his "inner life":

1. *Don't try to give your child a head start by encouraging him to watch television or "advanced" programming before he's ready.* "We've done some research that suggests that sometimes the first words that children speak are 'Big Bird' and 'Cookie Monster,'" Valeria Lovelace of "Sesame Street" points out. Personally, I'm partial to "Mama" and "Dada."

It's not surprising that parents are tempted to start their kids on "Sesame Street" long before it makes any sense. After all, if you're trying to create a superbaby, this is one of the most inexpensive and convenient means available—and besides, the local nursery school won't take your six-month-old! But it's silly to sell yourself on the idea that your child's brain cells are multiplying faster because you park his infant seat in front of the TV. A 1976 study reported that four-year-olds looked at the screen *four times* as long as one-year-olds while watching "Sesame Street." And according to Dr. Lovelace, the show is aimed at children aged three to five, with four the target audience.

Studies show that before the age of two and one-half, a child is unlikely to sit down and deliberately watch TV. He doesn't understand much of what's shown, because he lacks the life experience and cognitive awareness to do so. He'll learn more if you leave off the set and offer him the opportunity to explore the real world—which is what he really wants to do, anyway. "Television shouldn't be the major part of a child's growing up," says ACT president Peggy Charren. "For young children television is not terribly productive. Wait until you feel you *have* to turn it on." When is that? Preferably at the earliest, when your child is old enough to be able to *ask* to watch. Plant your eight-month-old in front of "Sesame Street" and he's unlikely to learn the ABCs. In fact, he'll probably just lag behind in verbal development, because he needs live *people* to talk with. Toddlers are generally far too busy exploring every corner of their environment—as well they should be—to spend much time gazing at the screen. Don't try to sit them down in front of "3–2–1 Contact"; offer them a few plastic containers and let them explore physics at the kitchen sink.

Around age two and one-half, a child is still discovering the wonders of his world, but this point marks the beginning of a transition to a level of symbolic thinking at which he becomes more capable of comprehending action on a two-dimensional screen (as opposed to objects in hand). This is the stage when you can encourage his fledgling attempts at pretend play by providing dress-up clothes, blocks, a tea set, miniature figures, and household objects that he can use as props in his fantasies. He'll soon be creating an imaginary world far more satisfying and exciting to him than anything he'd see on the screen. But at this early symbolic stage, *if he asks to watch TV,* he will have a better grasp of what's being shown. It's up to you to help him begin to develop intelligent viewing habits right from the start.

This means choosing shows that make sense for his age and personality. Once your child does start watching television, studies have shown that it's important to match the program with his level of understanding. No show is right for all kids all the time. "Sarah watched 'Sesame Street' from the time she was a year old to about eighteen months, two or three times a week," one mother told me. "And then there was a character that came out of a swimming pool wearing diving fins. And Sarah said, 'Turn it off, I'm afraid.' That was the end of 'Sesame Street.' "

A beginning television viewer will feel most comfortable with a show featuring a central adult figure who appears to address the child personally, helps introduce and interpret the material, and provides a sense of warmth and stability—someone like Captain Kangaroo or Mister Rogers. " 'Mister Rogers' Neighborhood' is a good show, *if* a child is going to watch television, because he talks to the children and it's very slow and consistent," says Margaret Bloodgood of the City and Country School, adding quickly, "But it's still television—it'd still be better not to watch anything. There's no question about *that.*"

2. *Plan your child's television viewing.* This means both *limiting* and *selecting* his programs. By helping your child choose certain shows he wants to see, and agreeing on a limited number in advance, you can help him develop his critical faculties— and avoid battles. Setting limits on viewing is a basic recommendation of Action for Children's Television. And keep in mind that, as Valeria Lovelace says, "in some of the research it would appear that ten hours a week of television viewing has some kind of positive effect on children's learning—exposure to letters and numbers, vocabulary building, and so on . . . but after that, it seems to interfere with the time that children have for other activities. . . . reading, sports activities, riding bicycles, and things like that."

If you do decide to allow him to watch only an hour a day, what can you do if he's already hooked on three different shows? Try drawing up a chart on which you agree that programs will be watched on alternate days. Child psychologists also suggest that each time he watches you help him choose a show to match his mood: "Mister Rogers' Neighborhood" might be soothing to a child who's had a busy day, for example, while "Sesame Street" could pep up a rainy afternoon.

Needless to say, when no one's watching, the set should be off. Child psychologist Lawrence Balter, Ph.D., suggests putting it away or closing it behind cabinet doors, just as you'd return a book to its shelf after reading.

And don't interpret the frequent airings of "Sesame Street" on your PBS station as an invitation to park Justin and Sarah in front of it every time it's on. "Action for Children's Television is in favor of having a variety of times to air everything," says Peggy Charren. "But because a show is aired four times a day doesn't mean the parent's supposed to sit the child in front of it four times a day. If you're out in the morning, then you can catch it in the afternoon."

3. *Be available to your child while he's watching TV.* You've probably read advice from experts telling you to sit down and watch TV with your child. In the real world, with laundry to load, dishes to clear, and bills to pay, most parents feel they deserve at least an hour a day to try and accomplish such tasks. But do try to stay within earshot so that you can answer your child's questions about the programs and know what he's watched. Just as you interpret reality for him when you go for a walk together ("That's a cherry tree. Can you guess what will grow on it after those flowers fade?"), you're his guide in televisionland. Rather than getting annoyed at his questions ("Be quiet and watch the show!") be grateful that he's resisting the widespread tendency to turn into a zombie in front of the set, and answer as best you can.

How important is this? Well, one research group reanalyzed the data from the ETS "Sesame Street" study and argued that kids whose mothers became involved with the series showed greater gains than did the control group in which mothers were not encouraged to become involved, even though the children watched the same number of episodes per week. "Having a parent there does facilitate learning from 'Sesame Street,' so we want to encourage that type of behavior," says Valeria Lovelace. "That's the reason why, from the very beginning, we've had celebrities on 'Sesame Street.' They're not child celebrities. They're adult celebrities, and that's so that the mother or father might hear their favorite artist and come into the room, or might see their favorite sports star, and say, 'Oh, my gosh, what's *he* doing there, teaching about the letter *A?*' "

Remaining nearby also gives you the chance to notice whether your child is becoming frightened or irritable as a result of the show—a good time to turn off the set and do something quiet together. For a young child, the dividing line between reality and fantasy is blurry, to say the least, and even seemingly innocuous scenes can be scary.

4. Consider whether each program is suited to your child's particular style of learning. Just because a show is supposed to teach reading or science, or is shown on educational television, that doesn't guarantee that it will teach *your* child a blessed thing. Just as different kids enjoy different books and toys, they have their preferences about TV. This isn't just a matter of personality, but of how your child approaches learning.

Dr. Edward Chittendon of ETS has studied the different styles and strategies kids use when they're trying to make sense out of their world. According to his findings, they tend to fall into two main categories: Some children have a narrow scope of attention, pay a great deal of attention to details, and seem to think in linear sequence, solving problems step-by-step. "These are kids who are really focused, who take one thing at a time and go into it at some depth," he explains. "Then there are kids who process things in parallel, who can handle a lot of stuff coming in from all different directions and don't seem to mind it."

Those in the latter group can better juggle diverse information and, he suggests, are more likely to feel at home on "Sesame Street." If your child is the "focusing" kind, he might prefer Mister Rogers or an old-fashioned story. Try a thirty-minute videotape based on one of his favorite books.

5. Use television as a takeoff point for hands-on activities in your child's life, not as a substitute for them. One reason many parents have their kids watch TV is that they believe that it offers a chance to see distant or offbeat places they don't encounter in everyday life. But just as watching "Magnum, P.I." is a long way from actually lying on a beach under the Hawaiian sun with Tom Selleck, a TV sequence on maple sugaring is no trip to Vermont. For an experience to be vivid and meaningful to a young child, he needs to use all his senses—feel the bark of the maple tree and smell and taste the sap dripping into the bucket.

In order really to bring these video visits to life for him, you need to incorporate them into your child's day. In fact, Yale University's Jerome and Dorothy Singer have found that many parents can actually *encourage* imagination and language use by planning activities in conjunction with television viewing. Children's Television Workshop puts out *Sesame Street* magazine for the purpose, but there's no reason to make your child believe Bert and Ernie have cornered the market on knowledge of the universe. In fact, some adult programming—such as sports broadcasts, nature shows, or documentaries—can also serve as a start-off point for fun with your child. You might watch the weather forecaster on the news and have your child guess whether he's going to be right about tomorrow's rain. This gives you a chance to talk about the sun, clouds, rain, the passage of time, and so on.

Don't worry that you have to start doing elaborate arts-and-crafts or science projects, either. "It should be as natural as the show," says Valeria Lovelace. "If in watching the show you see something, and you go to a grocery store and can connect the child's experience there with what he saw on television, then that's very concrete and happening in the child's life right now. Then the next time your child sees it on 'Sesame Street,' you've made a bridge."

To build that bridge, just follow these three simple steps designed to bring television subject matter to life for your child:

■ *Take notice of what particularly interests your child about a TV episode.* Wonderful though it may be that the renowned cellist Yo-Yo Ma is visiting Mister Rogers, if your child becomes intrigued by the idea of wearing a cardigan sweater that day, don't force the music issue. "Sometimes with young children, they don't see the central message in the first exposure," says Dr. Lovelace. "We may be teaching about the elephant at the zoo, and for some reason this child is hung up on the hose. The next time that child may see something else." If you want him to become active and involved, build on whatever has sparked *his* imagination.

■ *Try to offer him a real object related to the topic and give him the opportunity to explore it however he likes.* Let him try on one of your sweaters; he may get excited about playing dress-up. Offer him the chance to taste real maple syrup on a pancake or waffle. If Bert and Ernie plant seeds, you can, too. And if "Sesame Street" visits a crayon factory, bring out his Crayolas. If you're both in the mood for an outing, aim for something that will encourage his interest in what he has seen—a visit to the gardening center to buy some seeds and walk through the greenhouse, a visit to a knitting shop, or a morning at a nature center at maple-sugaring time.

■ *Encourage your child to share his impressions about what he's watched, just as you'd compare notes with your spouse after a movie.* What was the most interesting thing he saw at the peanut-butter factory? Did the puppets remind him of the ones you both saw a few weeks ago in the park? Be careful not to interrogate him; instead, gently respond to his interest by listening attentively and answering his questions. Build on his interest by telling him something else *you* know about the topic. ("Do you know what's inside a seed?")

Keep in mind that some kids prefer to wait and talk a short while after the show is over, once they've had a chance to digest it or even talk it over to themselves. As with every aspect of child-rearing, the key is to be sensitive to your own child and allow him to grow and unfold as a person in his own unique way.

The Video Alternative

For the past few years there's been a revolution brewing in children's access to television. As increasing numbers of parents have purchased videocassette recorders, many are using this new technology to take a more creative approach to viewing. Assuming you don't use the tape as a hypnotic device that your child watches hour after hour ("My son's starting to talk like Mister Rogers," one mother grumbled to me), videotaping is a fresh opportunity to put you and your child in control of the set. "There's some very entertaining stuff in the home video market for preschoolers, and I think that's something that didn't exist in the preschool market when I started out," says Peggy Charren. "With video, the only concern is how much time the kid spends in front of that television set, because that's still a problem—even if it's wonderful home video."

There are several significant advantages to using a VCR:

■ You can control *when* your kids watch television. One of the most insidious ways television takes control of a home is by being inflexible. If you want to watch a particular show, you'd better be sitting in front of the set at three o'clock sharp. Kids learn very early that the set has power over them. But with the VCR, you can make the television wait for *you.* Your kids can enjoy the old-fashioned childhood luxury of carefree hours climbing trees, finger painting, and playing dress-up without worrying that they're missing their latest favorite.

You may also find you cut down on battles about how much TV your child watches, thanks to the simple fact that *a videotape comes to an end.* American television, by contrast, is a perpetual motion machine, and kids know there's always "something on" after every show.

■ You can control *what* your kids watch on television. For once that doesn't mean telling them what *not* to watch; whether you buy or rent tapes, or borrow them from the public library, you can help your kids select from an ever-increasing variety of videotapes, from Disney to *Little Toot* to *Charlotte's Web.*

Many children's book publishers (such as Scholastic and Random House) have set up video divisions, and they make a creditable attempt to present stories designed to appeal to a child's imagination. At our house, for example, *Changes, Changes,* an animated view of block-building in which blocks are transformed into everything, from boats to trucks, presented by an enthusiastic adult moderator, was quite a hit and seemed to inspire my son to reach new heights (literally) with his own wooden blocks. Interactive videos (such as Video-Smarts, from Connor Toys) offer the child an opportunity to press buttons on a controller in response to questions asked on the screen. Currently there is a lopsided emphasis on the ABCs and numbers, but the technology holds promise for the future.

Keep in mind that parent participation is just as important with videos as with broadcast TV. For one thing, it's up to you to keep your child from being frightened by a tape. Try to *preview* the video (just as you'd leaf through a children's book at the library or bookstore) before offering it to your child; this is often worthwhile because some of the best-known classics are surprisingly scary. If you're renting, ask the video-store personnel for guidance; our local shop attaches brief critical notes to tapes, saying things like "Warning: Sad Story!" And don't assume a tape is okay just because you've read the book; our Matthew loved the book *Little Toot* but began to cry during the video, when violent waves were tossing boats around at sea.

You can also encourage interest in reading via videos. "If you use the tape to get your kids interested in the book, and keep in your head someplace that eventually reading books may be more satisfying than watching somebody else's video, it can be a very nice activity," observes Peggy Charren. Take your cue from the approach used by many classroom teachers and coordinate your library selections with your videos. As your child watches the video of *Winnie-the-Pooh,* for example, you can point out details that diverge from the original book. And at storytime, when you get to a part of the story that your child found especially entertaining on video, you can remind him: "Didn't Winnie look funny doing his exercises?"

■ You can control *how* your kids watch television. The use of videos gives them an opportunity to watch a program more than once, just the way they'd listen to a story or play a record. Each time they'll notice a new aspect of the story and understand a little bit more. If they ask a question part way through, you also have the option of pressing the stop button—just as you'd wait before turning the page of a book—to give them a full explanation.

According to Peggy Charren, young children often come to feel possessive about a favorite videotape. "They walk around holding it the way kids in my generation used to hold a book," she says. "And they learn very fast the use of the buttons. They'll push the tape until they find the part they like. They will look at it over and over the way they would ask a grown-up to reread a good story." This is quite unlike the "nonreflective viewing stance" Jerome and Dorothy Singer of Yale warn against.

Obviously, we'd all like to have our children avoid all "nonreflective" television viewing, but there are times when family life seems to demand the palliative presence of an ordinary rerun. "Sesame Street" is certainly one of TV's better baby-sitters. Some of the high-quality videos also fall into this category. But it's a mistake to assume that because one hour per day is harmless, four hours are highly educational. The preschool child is above all an explorer whose tools are his five senses and who is driven by his natural curiosity to understand the world. Vegging out in front of the set, no matter what's on the air, is still vegging out. It is only when television encourages children's efforts to learn for themselves that it can truly be called "educational."

If You Play the Piano While You're Pregnant, Will You Have a Prodigy?

Expectant father (playing the clarinet and xylophone to his wife's bulging belly): "Can baby hear A sharp? Can baby hear D flat? Can baby understand 'Juilliard scholarship, summa cum laude'??!"

—*From the "Cathy" comic strip, by Cathy Guisewite*

ON THE SURFACE it's hard to see what could be wrong with teaching music to your budding Beethoven. After all, even the youngest infant enjoys the sound of music, from her rattle and squeaky toy to the wind-up mobile that plays Brahms's "Lullabye." And didn't most of the great composers start young? Felix Mendelssohn's mother, herself an amateur musician, started him on the piano at three. Mozart also played the piano at three, and was already composing at six. And the twentieth-century composer Benjamin Britten begged to "pay pano" as young as two years of age, and was reading symphony and opera scores to himself at bedtime by the time he was seven.

On the other hand, Gustav Mahler only discovered the piano at the age of six, when he found one in his grandmother's attic and busied himself with figuring out the keyboard. Richard Wagner didn't start on the instrument until he was fifteen, and George Gershwin, who heard his first live jazz performance as late as six, didn't take piano lessons until the ripe old age of twelve.

But the musical consequences of early beginnings are not the whole story. As anyone who saw Peter Schaffer's acclaimed musical portrait of Mozart, *Amadeus,* knows, children of every era pushed into the role of prodigy have often led unhappy and even tragic lives. Once young Wolfgang knew his way around the piano, his father lost no time in taking him on tour and teaching him a few showbiz tricks—how to play a clavier whose keyboard was covered with a cloth, for example. But for the rest of his life, young Wolfgang lagged way behind his peers in anything *not* related to music. He failed to pick up such basic survival skills as how to manage his money or his career, and when he died, in debt, at the age of thirty-five, he was buried in an unmarked grave. Mozart's first biographer, Friedrich Schlichtegroll, summed it up two years later, in 1793: "For just as this rare being early became a man so far as his art was concerned, he always remained—as the impartial observer must say of him—in almost all other matters a child."

Mozart, at least, was a genius. An ordinary kid with a lopsided upbringing and less talent would have fared even worse, no doubt. That's why, before you sign your preschooler up for formal lessons on a musical instrument, it's worth stopping to ask yourself, What am I trying to achieve?

■ Are you trying to turn your child into a virtuoso, in hopes she'll grow up to be rich and famous? If so, realize that when it comes to opportunities and pay, music is not exactly commodities trading. All but a fortunate few music students end up giving lessons to the next generation of hopeful little Paganinis. In his autobiography, *Joys and Sorrows* (1970), Pablo Casals tells of how his father, a church organist, "did not believe I could earn a living as a musician; he knew from experience how hard it was to do this. He thought it would be more practical for me to have a trade; and, in fact, when I was still a youngster he made plans with a carpenter friend for me to become his apprentice."

■ Do you want your child to cultivate a taste for string quartets or opera, rather than, say, punk or country music? "My three-year-old's latest favorite is 'Like a Virgin,' " moaned a working mother whose nanny often listens to Madonna records. Not to worry, musically speaking. *Any* music your child enjoys—from Sousa marches to Raffi to the theme song of "Mister Rogers"—will contribute to her musical awareness and, most important, her motivation. The folk singer Tom Glazer, whose songs (from "On Top of Spaghetti" to "Music for 1's and 2's") have provided generations of children with their earliest musical experiences, agrees: "Rock is bad if it's too loud or if it interferes with other activities during the day. But I think *any* kind of music that the parents like is better than no music at all. Rock is like any other form of music—there is good rock, there is bad rock, there is terrible rock. There is good classical music, there is bad classical music, there is indifferent classical music."

■ Do you want your child to learn an instrument at an early age because you believe that is when it comes "naturally" and "easily"? As we'll see when we discuss the Suzuki method (to borrow a phrase from a Gershwin song), it ain't necessarily so.

Let's face it: Only a small minority of our kids are destined for the concert stage. No matter when you start her on lessons, you're not going to end up with Alicia de Larrocha unless your child shows extraordinary talent and motivation *within herself.* Now, there is some speculation that the study of music may develop a capacity for intuitive thinking that can help children in whatever field they choose to pursue. In *Nurtured by Love* (1969), for example, Shinichi Suzuki quotes his friend Albert Einstein as saying that the revolutionary idea of the optics of motion "occurred to me by intuition. And music is the driving force behind this intuition. My parents had me study the violin from the time I was six. My new discovery is the result of musical perception."

But if early musical training leads few children to careers playing in recital halls, an even smaller number turn out to be Einsteins. That's why in the long run, the only sensible reason to introduce a child to music at an early age is "because it gives pleasure," as Tom Glazer puts it. Long before they can read or even speak enough to appreciate stories and poems, children can respond to and enjoy music. In his 1964 book *Tom Glazer's Treasury of Children's Songs,* the folk singer sums it up with a quotation from a 1917 book entitled *Music and Life,* by Thomas W. Surette:

> My object is therefore to suggest, first, that the perception of beauty is in the highest sense education. Second, that music is especially so, because it is the purest form of beauty. And third, that music is the only form of beauty by means of which very young children can be educated. It is the only form accessible to them.

And study after study shows that children who grow up with music in the home learn to love it. As researchers at the University of Houston discovered when testing 201 second-grade children, the two factors most common among those with musical awareness were that at least one of their parents sang *to* them, and sang *with* them. From an early age, many also had toy musical instruments, toys that made noise, and a musical parent (one who helped the child learn songs, provided recordings which the child was allowed to play without permission, or sang or played in a musical group).

Likewise, a 1981 study of individuals who had demonstrated the "highest levels of accomplishment" in various artistic fields, including music, found that in most cases one or more of their parents had a strong personal interest in the field and, especially while they were between the ages of three and seven, had always offered them plenty of encouragement and support, inviting them to participate and turning it into a family pursuit.

Before you decide to turn your playroom into a rehearsal hall, though, remember that the parents in these studies had a genuine *love* of the art they taught their children. As Tom Glazer says of his two sons, now grown, "Neither of my sons is a professional musician, but they both play guitar and sing. I never sat down and taught them to play guitar, but they both play because they saw it around the house." Parents like Glazer do not decide to start listening to music or playing it for the sake of their children's education, but instead get the rest of the family excited simply through the strength of their personal passion. Merely going through the motions isn't worth the effort—unless it's fun for both of you, forget it. "When a child is entertained and pleased, he or she will learn something," says Glazer. "When somebody is singing 'The Eensy Weensy Spider,' and acting it out with their fingers, that is sheer joy to a child. You're giving them a very pleasant experience that starts with the natural love that you have for your child and your child has for you."

Born Musical

Today's mothers are so eager to introduce their offspring to the glories of music that they are even doing "belly broadcasts" of classical recordings to their unborn babies, holding stereo speakers under their maternity clothes. But there is no scientific evidence to support prenatal concerts as a method of breeding musical talent. I'll never forget the first time after the birth of my son that I heard the Pachelbel "Kanon" on the radio. During prenatal exercise classes, the instructor had always played this piece as a relaxation technique, encouraging us to imagine and love our babies as we cradled them in our bellies. Now, holding my six-week-old baby in my arms, I blinked back tears at the memory and looked at him expectantly. Guess what? Utterly unmoved, he continued sucking blithely away on his pacifier (not even keeping time to the music!).

Nonetheless, even a newborn can appreciate music *when it is an integral part of a loving parent-child relationship.* Many experts believe that music comes as naturally to children as speech, as long as the child's musical expressions are encouraged by a responsive parent. An important study of the spontaneous musical activities of young children two to six years old was launched by the Pillsbury Foundation in 1937. After several years, the authors of the study concluded that in a child's life music is "not an isolated thing, it is part of a life-process; it is separate neither from the child's consciousness nor from any aspect of . . . everyday life . . . For the child . . . lives, and makes music." Whether she's banging two blocks together, clapping her hands, or even whining, a young child is constantly expressing herself musically.

As a 1973 study suggested, all the elements of music are present in a newborn's first cry. Sucking and babbling, for example, represent in part the baby's first experiments with rhythm. Therefore, the study concluded, musical development should evolve by means of social interaction, just as speech does.

In the important University of Chicago study *Developing Talent in Young People* (1985), edited by Benjamin S. Bloom, which examined the lives of 120 highly talented people in various fields, the researchers found that music was a natural part of the concert pianists' lives "almost from birth." And even when they were very young, the children were praised for their attempts at music-making: "The early years of learning were playful and filled with immediate rewards. . . . Much attention, praise, and applause were given to the children's musical efforts," writes research coordinator Lauren Sosniak, Ph.D. "It was an interest parents could share with their child and an opportunity for parents and children to play together and feel a closeness with one another."

If you genuinely enjoy music, you can expose your child to it and encourage her efforts to make music of her own, as another researcher found:

. . . the first essential condition favoring the full development of musical ability in the earliest years is the opportunity to hear music. No doubt it is highly desirable that some
of this music should be made by a parent or other person
of whom the child is fond. But if the parents cannot play or
sing, they can at least try to listen to music with enjoyment
and attention, and show appreciation of music and musicians. Before he is old enough for formal music lessons, the
child can be encouraged to make his own music, with his
own voice and with whatever sound-producing facilities his
environment can offer.
—R. Shuter, *The Psychology of Musical Ability* (1968)

Other researchers have pointed out that even the tiniest infants
will lie still and listen to the sound of singing or the playing of
an instrument, and that a tune can work just as well as a teddy
bear as a comfort object. When our daughter, Laura, was less
than six months old, we carried along a tape of "All Through the
Night" on all overnight trips. Seven bars into the lullaby, she'd
be out like a light. It even helped her make the time change on
a trip to Europe.

As your baby grows, her babbling will sometimes break into
a chant (usually while she's absorbed in her toys), which marks
what educators term her "first spontaneous musical expression."
My son's favorite number at the agreeable age of two went like
this: "No, no, no, no./No, no, no, no." At two your child may
be able to sing song phrases back to you, although usually not
on pitch. Keep singing those nursery rhymes and playing those
tapes, though, and by three she'll be singing her versions of
whole songs (still probably off-key). By four, she'll belt out
entire songs correctly.

According to an early landmark study, a child's first songs and
chants rarely exceed three measures and often consist of repeti-
tions of the same tune. Researchers observed that children sang
most often when playing alone, and especially when involved in
rhythmic activity (such as hammering).

Suzuki, or not Suzuki?

"You're training, nitty-gritty training. This is not just a
pleasant little afternoon activity. If you can't accept that, go
sign them up for a music appreciation course."

—Suzuki teacher

If you can help develop your child's musical abilities by playing
an instrument yourself, making available a good supply of recordings, and encouraging her to make music, the Suzuki method would appear to be a foolproof recipe. This is a method that
requires the parent to put in even more work than her child, at
least for the first few years. The thousands of parents around the
world whose kids enter the program, devised by Dr. Shinichi Suzuki of Japan at the end of World War II, attend weekly classes in
violin, piano, or cello (so that they will be able to set an example
for their Shirley Temple and understand her difficulties firsthand) and attend their child's private and group lessons, as well
as "festivals," or group recitals. At home, they're in charge of getting the child to practice—which can entail playing tapes of the
lessons, keeping a progress chart, and playing along with her.

As Suzuki conceived the approach, it is based on loving interaction between parent and child. In his book *Nurtured by Love*
Suzuki illustrates his philosophy by describing a three-year-old
girl, Hitomi Kasuya, who happily practiced the violin for *three
hours* every day. "Hitomi's mother brought her a violin instead
of a doll and played a record of the piece to be studied over and
over again as a kind of background music," he explains. "Hitomi
played with the violin all day, as if it were a toy. Her mother
would now and then show her the correct way to play, according
to our instructions, letting Hitomi think she was playing a game
with her. This is the art of education at its best."

Kids Will Be Kids

Unfortunately, when this approach is adapted for use with
American three-year-olds and their moms en masse, more than

a little spontaneity gets lost in the translation. Once parents are subsidizing their preschoolers' music lessons to the tune of over one thousand dollars a year, they're bound to expect a return on their investment. As a result, things get a little more businesslike. At one major Suzuki school, for example, the parent is instructed that her role as a "surrogate teacher" requires "working every day with the child at home," attending all the child's lessons (usually three per week in addition to the parents' class), and "observing, taking notes, and conferring with the teacher on how best to practice with the child." So much for fun and games.

And if you dream of hearing the Tchaikovsky Violin Concerto wafting through your home, listen to this, from the same school's brochure: "All pieces to be learned are to be transferred from the record to a tape, recorded as many times as possible on one or two sides of a sixty-minute tape, or transferred to a three- or six-minute endless tape. When learning a new piece, the child is asked to listen to this repetitive tape for as much as two hours a day." And we're talking "Twinkle, Twinkle, Little Star."

In theory, assuming the child manages to stay awake through all this repetition, she picks up music naturally—the way the children of Osaka learn to speak the difficult Osaka dialect, as Suzuki puts it. Music and violin-playing become second nature to her. That doing something often or repeatedly creates talent is a highly dubious assumption, of course, as Lauren A. Sosniak points out in a chapter of *Developing Talent in Young People:* "People do spend many years engaged in an activity (cooking, typing, or teaching, for example) without ever learning to do it well." Furthermore, in practice, the Suzuki method is highly structured and requires more discipline than many young American children (and their parents) seem to have.

In one Suzuki class of four-year-olds I visited, despite the instructor's best efforts to appeal to the kids at their own level (having them sing "like sirens," and hold their bows vertically like "helicopters in the air") they persisted in behaving like— you guessed it—kids. "Robert, would you get on your feet, please?" the teacher admonished one student who felt the urge to nap. "You don't lie down during your lesson time." Another child put down his violin and reached up to hug his mother, who visibly tensed up. "Quick! The teacher's going to come take away your violin!" she hissed, keeping him at arm's length and pressing the instrument back into his hand. "She's going to put it in the closet if you don't start playing!"

During the mothers' group lesson, after the moms scrape through "Happy Birthday," they discuss the problem of getting their reluctant prodigies to concentrate on the task at hand. "They say 'Yes, yes, yes,' and they're a million miles away. It's the old passive resistance tool," observes the teacher. The mothers, half of them pregnant, look weary. One of them yawns widely without bothering to cover her mouth. After they play "Twinkle, Twinkle, Little Star," the teacher talks with each mother about her child's particular brand of rebellion. Far from being an "effortless" or "natural" approach, this particular program seems to require constant cajoling to get the child to participate during class and practice at home, using a system of rewards, peer pressure, and pop psychology.

This high cost in effort isn't too surprising, particularly in light of a 1975 New Zealand report on the most effective ways to teach music to preschoolers. "Many younger children find it difficult to tolerate large-group activities for more than a very short time," write the researchers. "It is best, therefore, not to confine music to a planned, rigidly scheduled music period. Rather, music should be encouraged and incorporated as a specific part of many daily activities, including science, language, and movement exploration." Asking a group of three- or four-year-olds to pay attention for an hour and a half of music classes (brief private lesson, group lesson, and eurhythmics), all at the same time, in the same room, at the same hour every week, is expecting a lot.

And expecting your child to abandon the sandbox for the concert stage is unrealistic, too—as Suzuki himself has pointed out again and again. For Suzuki, who developed his method in war-torn Japan, encouraging children to make beautiful music and enjoy it is nothing less than a path to world peace. In *Nurtured by Love,* he emphasizes that the purpose of the lessons is to help the child

> become a noble person through his violin playing. Isn't that good enough? You should stop wanting your child to become a professional, a good money earner. This thought . . . is offensive. A person with a fine and pure heart will find happiness. The only concern for parents should be to bring up their children as noble human beings. That is sufficient. *If this is not their greatest hope, in the end the child may take a road contrary to their expectations* [italics added].

Unfortunately, says Lorraine Fink, a Suzuki teacher and the editor of *Suzuki World* magazine (with subscribers in thirty-four countries), parents who flock to Suzuki do not tend to share this world view. "It does attract the stage mother, the high achiever. Suzuki spends most of his time pressing people not to push their children," she says. "Too many people take the method and ignore the philosophy, which is the main thing."

It's hard to imagine the average parent paying such large sums to teach her child an instrument and not expecting *some* kind of return on her investment. After all, surely we can turn our kids into "noble human beings" by showing them sunsets for free?

If you *do* decide to try the Suzuki method with your child, be forewarned that not all Suzuki programs are alike. "Most Suzuki programs are not very good," admits Lorraine Fink. "The individual teacher makes all the difference in the world. A lot of teachers have not learned how to work with children when they're four and five years old."

No matter how patient the teacher, don't expect your child to play Bach fugues by the age of four. Preschoolers have so much to learn about following directions and taking turns that these lessons often take precedence over the musical ones. "The trick is, don't push too much too soon," says Eleanor Wortley, director of the Suzuki program at the Westchester Conservatory in

White Plains, New York, and a Suzuki teacher for thirty years. "If they can hold the instrument and bow, and play rhythms on the open strings, that's pretty much par for the course for three-year-olds."

If, despite all those lessons, your preschooler would rather take her violin to the junkyard than Juilliard, don't despair. "People bring these precocious children and think they're going to be marvelous musicians," says Wortley. "These parents tend to be very head-oriented people. But the child who does well with an instrument at this age tends to be the one who's physically coordinated. It has nothing to do with how smart they are." Why not find out what she's *really* interested in, and encourage her in that direction? You never know what might happen. In Arthur Rubinstein's *My Young Years* (1973), the renowned pianist wrote of his father's determination to switch him to the violin, when at the age of three he was already playing the piano by ear. "My father had a predilection for the violin; he found it more human, more distinguished than the piano. The success of a number of child prodigies also had impressed him. He presented me with a small fiddle, which I promptly smashed to pieces. And was spanked in return. He made another attempt to convince me of the superiority of the noble stringed instrument, but it definitely failed."

Sizing Up a Suzuki Program

To help you avoid the so-so Suzuki class, Lorraine Fink offers three criteria by which to judge whether a program is a good one, and right for your child:

1. Is your child *enjoying* the study? "He shouldn't necessarily love practicing the violin more than going swimming," says Fink, "but he shouldn't have to be dragged kicking and screaming to practice, either."

2. Is group time a *happy* time? "He should go home saying, 'Gee, I had fun today. I want to learn to play that piece better!' "

3. Does the instructor encourage parents *not* to compare their children's playing with that of others, and not to criticize their progress? "We have to constantly remind parents not to say to their kids as they're driving home in the car, 'Well, so-and-so started lessons around the same time as you and look how well *she* plays," says Fink.

Healthy Ways to Help

"Music is an important part of our home life. I always sang to my daughter a great deal when she was an infant. Then, when she was eleven months, we realized that she was humming 'Baa, Baa, Black Sheep' on pitch. We tried to encourage her in fun, hands-on ways, but we tried to keep it low-key. Now that she's eight, she actually likes to practice the piano—she does it in the morning before school!"
        —*Piano teacher whose daughter plays violin and piano*

In many ways, the growth of musical awareness is very similar to the development of reading readiness. By offering your child frequent opportunities to *enjoy* music, and plenty of materials with which to *make* music (just as you read aloud to her and provide crayons, paper, and magnetic letters), you can encourage her to listen with pleasure, and to express herself musically. If she is unusually talented, say most experts, she'll quickly let you know. And if not, she'll get a good start on a lifetime of musical pleasure and the two of you will have a great time together.

The key is to relax and do what comes naturally—sing, play an instrument or a recording, even tap out a rhythm on the kitchen table. "It's not *what* you teach but *how* you teach it that counts," says the folk singer Tom Glazer. "To do music with children is another form of love. It's the relationship that's important, and when that is there, the rest will follow."

To get you started, here are some guidelines to help you and your child enjoy music together at each stage of early childhood:

■ With an *infant,* do plenty of singing and talking. At this age, she is aware of *timbre,* or the quality of sound (the difference between a flute and a tuba, for example) and will enjoy lots of variety. Let your baby hear all the fascinating sounds her world has to offer in the course of a day—the tick tock of a clock, the click of a metronome, music boxes, automobile horns, church bells, wind chimes, squeaky toys, lullabies on tape. A baby can hear the voice on the other end of the telephone, see and touch the doorbell, and watch you play the guitar or even a kazoo. Just as important, when *she* makes a sound—from a syllable to a clap to a sneeze—offer plenty of praise and feedback. Don't feel obliged to barrage her with music; think of yourselves as a duet.

■ Your *two- or three-year-old* delights in moving to music—as energetically as possible, although not necessarily on the beat. At this age, acquiring a repertoire of creative movements rather than drilling in keeping time is the important thing. Encourage your child to move her body to the lyrics of a song, such as "Jack and Jill." Play a lively tune and watch her clap, dance, and parade around the room. She'll also enjoy experimenting with *dynamics,* singing very softly or very loudly.

If you worry that she's singing like a broken record, keep in mind that one study found that young children "often focus upon one prominent feature of a song, perhaps a repeated melodic or rhythmic phrase." Offer applause, provide props such as scarves and rhythm instruments, teach her short songs with a strong beat (nursery rhymes are great), and join in the dancing when the spirit moves you.

■ *Older three- and four-year-olds* like to learn songs (or fragments thereof) and act out stories to music. They're exploring timbre when they imitate animal sounds—a lion's roar or a bird's chirp, for example. At this age, their idea of pitch has improved, although they may fall out of key midway through a song, only to return to the right pitch at the end.

Preschoolers love to play instruments, but that doesn't mean you have to figure piano payments into the family budget. "My first instrument was a kazoo," says Tom Glazer. "In fact, it wasn't even a kazoo. Somebody showed me when I was five years old that you could put tissue paper around a comb, and I thought that was a fascinating sound. Then I got a little harmonica. Later on, I started on the ukelele. We didn't have a piano at home." Glazer advises steering clear of instruments that look real but emit only toneless thumps or squeaks. "Toy instruments are fine if they're musical instruments," he suggests, "but not if they're cheap plastic imitations. That may turn the child off for a lifetime!" Many parents have found the portable electronic keyboards sold for the adult market to be a better value—and produce a less tinny sound—than toy pianos.

■ *Four- and five-year-olds* have a longer attention span and may be interested in listening more carefully. They often enjoy musical stories, like Prokofiev's *Peter and the Wolf,* Dukas's *The Sorcerer's Apprentice,* and Saint-Saëns's *Carnival of the Animals.*

At this age, your child may enjoy participating in a group music program. Check to see if her nursery school incorporates music into the day's activities (it's an integral part of traditional nursery schools, but the "academic" kind sometimes downplay it). Or (assuming her day isn't already too busy) sign her up for a class at the local YMCA, boys' club, or other recreation center. Churches sometimes have preschool singing groups or "cherub choirs." Naturally, how much fun she has, and what she learns, will depend on her individual inclinations and stage of development, as well as the style of the teacher.

Here are four methods commonly used to teach music to children in groups:

■ *Creative movement:* Through a dramatic, rhythmic, and expressive approach to dance, children gain a heightened awareness of their own bodies as well as the music. At its best, creative movement is not forty-five minutes of flitting around a room like so many Isadora Duncans in overalls. Instead, the teacher engages the children in a structured approach to moving their bodies, using varied rhythms, dynamics (loudness), tempos, and story themes.

■ *Dalcroze Eurhythmics:* With this time-honored approach, created by the Swiss composer Émile Jaques-Dalcroze, the children receive ear training by moving rhythmically to the music.

■ *Kodály method:* These classes teach music through folk singing, using a method devised by the Hungarian composer Zoltán Kodály. They start at the point where music breaks off from natural speech—in English, melodies based on the minor third (roughly equivalent to the familiar whine or teasing chant, "nyah-nyah-nyah-NYAH-nyah!"). The concept of pitch is physically reinforced by body movement, which the child learns to associate with higher or lower hand positions.

■ *Carl Orff's approach:* Orff, a German composer, incorporated movement and speech, as well as music, into his program for young children. Using specially designed xylophones and glockenspiels with removable tone bars (allowing the teacher to select a limited number of tones for each instrument), they can improvise accompaniments to songs.

Listen and Learn

Lacking the time, resources, or inclination to send your child to an organized program, you can make lots of beautiful music together at home. In fact, it's more likely to stick with your child if it becomes part of everyday life. One mother told me how she and her three-year-old daughter sing "Oats, and Beans, and Barley Grow," as they work in the vegetable garden.

Just listening to music is also fun. Does this mean family subscriptions to the opera? Not unless you can afford box seats so that your child has room to spread out her Legos on the floor. Except for outdoor music festivals, grown-up performances demand far too much sitting in one place for a preschooler. Some mothers of three- and four-year-olds report that their kids are beginning to appreciate ballet (especially *The Nutcracker*). But puppet shows and children's concerts, aimed at preschoolers' attention spans and goofy humor, are the most sensible way to teach your child how much pleasure music can give.

At home, play whatever music you and your child like. There is evidence to show that kids do learn to enjoy the types of music they hear regularly: a 1968 study published in the *Journal of Research in Music Education* found that nearly 50 percent of a group of four- to six-year-olds showed a slight change in preference toward jazz or classical music after they had been exposed to it repeatedly. Nonetheless, if you're not having fun, your child is bound to realize it. There's no point in having her listen to music you don't enjoy. (You'll have plenty of time for that later on when she's a teenager.)

As you're listening, picking out the various instruments by their sound can be fun, and a good way to develop your child's powers of observation, too. One study showed that three- and four-year-olds can often learn to recognize the various musical instruments by hearing them. But take care not to turn listening time into a highly serious guessing game that spoils the direct experience of the music. Just do what comes naturally, says

Glazer: "You simply play the record and wait for the child's reaction."

That doesn't mean playing the tape recorder all day, either, unless you want to produce a kind of Muzak for Munchkins that turns into background noise. "Whenever I do a concert, I always tell the children at some point to close their eyes and be quiet, because silence is a musical thing, too," says Glazer, "and it's very important for music to be a quiet experience in a noisy world."

Kids' Favorites, Old and New

Here's a partial list of records and performers loved by kids (and their parents) from birth to five. Although it begins with recordings for babies, kids can enjoy the same music in different ways at different ages. Naturally, they'll enjoy adult music, too.

"The Baby Record" (Kids' Records)

"Songs and Games for Toddlers" (Kids' Records)

Tom Glazer: "Music for 1's and 2's," "More Music for 1's and 2's (and 3's and 4's)," "Let's Sing Fingerplays, Activity and Game Songs" (CMS Records)

"Babysong" (Educational Activities, Inc., with Martha and Hap Palmer)

Rosenshontz: "Tickles You!" and "It's the Truth!" (RS Records)

"Peter, Paul, and Mommy" (Warner Bros.)

Burl Ives: "The Best of Burl Ives," vols. I and II, and "Greatest Hits" (MCA)

Malvina Reynolds: "Artichokes, Griddlecakes and Other Good Things" (Cassandra)

Raffi: "Singable Songs for the Very Young," "More Singable Songs," "Baby Beluga" (Troubadour Records)

Wee Sing: "Nursery Rhymes and Lullabyes," "Campfire Songs," "Wee Sing and Play" (Price/Stern/Sloan)

Carol Hammett and Elaine Bueffel: "It's Toddler Time," "Toddlers on Parade" (Kimbo Educational)

Ready for the Infant Olympics?

Aaron was only 2 years old, but not too young to climb a fence and fall in the family swimming pool. When his mother noticed he was missing, she rushed to the pool in panic. There she found her toddler confidently floating on his back . . .

[This] and other accidents could have resulted in fatal tragedies if their young victims had not been trained in water safety and survival. When we say a youngster is *watersafe*, we mean he can save his life if he accidentally falls in the water.

—*How to Watersafe Infants & Toddlers,* by Lana E. Whitehead and Lindsay R. Curtis, M.D., 1983

Your child's coordination, the ease and grace of his or her movements, the sensory-motor skills required for active living are almost completely determined at age 4.

—*Direct-mail advertisement for Playorena movement program*

IT'S HARD TO BELIEVE kids ever got their exercise at the playground. Visit your local YMCA, community recreation center, swimming pool, gymnastics club, or health club and you're more than likely to find a class or two for under-fives: Moms and Tots, Kidzercise, kindergym, Water Babies, Bubble Babies, and so on. You can buy books and videotapes to start your baby's swimming or exercise long before he gets his first pair of Weebocks. Our grandparents may have thought running, jumping, and climbing came naturally to little kids—that, if anything, they ought to be taught to stay *still* once in a while—but today's children, who are being formally trained in everything else, are getting lessons in how to move, too. "You can't learn about life in a playpen," warns the Gymboree movement program in its ads. "Kids genuinely enjoy playing and learning at Gymboree."

This is true, no doubt. After all, kids enjoy "playing and learning" just about *anywhere.* It's being stuck in one place and ignored—say, in a carseat—that drives them nuts. So can't they play and learn at home or in the park for free? Of course. In fact, the ad itself says "each 45-minute weekly class is filled with music, games, sights, and sounds they can experience at home." Lacking the inventiveness to teach your kid how to play "Simon says" or "pat-a-cake," you can pay the folks at Gymboree.

Admittedly, organized programs fill a very real function for *parents* in today's society. If you're a new mother who left the paid work force to care for your baby, enrolling in a Moms and Tots or infant swimming program can be a good way to meet other women like yourself. Many of today's trendy "new fathers" enjoy Saturday morning baby gym or swimming because it's a time for them to spend alone with baby—along with the eleven other daddy-baby pairs in the gym or pool, of course. "That's their special time together," one mother of a two-year-old told me, adding, "Besides, that way I get to sleep Saturday mornings!"

This is not to say many parents aren't sincerely concerned about their kids' physical development. After all, considering that nearly half the adults (43 percent) in this country say they exercise regularly, according to the National Center for Health Statistics, it's not surprising we're getting our kids into the act. With all the reports about how overweight and out of shape the youngest generation of Americans is, that's hardly a bad thing—although the most valuable exercise many children might do, according to a recent study reported in the *New England Journal of Medicine,* is get up and walk away from the TV.

Unfortunately, though, many parents are shelling out their six dollars a class for other reasons. For today's status-conscious moms and dads, it's simply not enough for a child to ride a tricycle in the driveway or climb the monkey bars in the local park. After all, a visit to the local health club is so much more appealing. "What we're seeing is that parents want adult-type activities," says Carol Totsky Hammett, an expert in children's movement who has produced several activity records for this age group, "and there are people in adult sport areas—swimming, gymnastics, et cetera—who are using programs intended for school-age children to meet the needs of preschoolers, and it just does not work."

When you're in a group of moms and toddlers, and everybody else's kid looks like a future Mary Lou Retton or Greg Louganis while *yours* is a tiny couch potato, it's hard not to give in to the pressure and start pushing. "My son screamed all the way through every class," recalled the mother of a seven-year-old who'd been signed up for swimming lessons at eighteen months. "But I allowed myself to be pressured by the other mothers, who all said *their* kids screamed when *they* started, and afterward they *loved* swimming. After three weeks, I couldn't take it, so I pulled him out. And I got one hundred percent disapproval from the other mothers. Guess what? He learned to swim at camp when he was five—painlessly."

Even if the peer pressure doesn't get you, there's the not-so-small matter of money. You pay the tuition fee or buy the books, and you expect to see results. Knowing this and wanting you to enroll for the next session, the instructor encourages your child to perform one new trick after another. Mom and Dad get exactly what they ask for, no matter how inappropriate for baby. "The business owner is in a tough situation because if you stick to your guns, in many instances your program is not viable financially. A lot of programs today are in existence because they are giving the parents what they want," says Hammett. "Many times the parents are uninformed—they're making the wrong decisions for their children—and the club owners are just going along with it." Who loses? The Absorba-clad athlete, of course.

Do We Need to Teach Kids How to Move?

Parents and children are both losers when so much of the fun and spontaneity goes out of what once was simply called *playing* with your child—rolling a ball back and forth with your infant on the living-room floor, or racing up and down the hallway, for example. Let's take a look at the structured exercises recommended for babies under three months of age in *The Baby Exercise Book* by Janine Levy (1974):

Strengthening the Thighs
Position: The child flat on his back on the ground or on the table.

With hands cupped behind the child's knees, by tossing very slowly and gently, straighten the legs and spread them apart.

Aim: To make the inner muscles of the thigh more supple while stretching them out and relaxing them.

Isn't it amazing to think that generations of newborns have managed to acquire sufficient strength and suppleness in their thighs to walk *without* such exercises? That babies are born with the capacity to develop the muscles they need in the normal course of an infant's day? That even babies in parts of Africa who are carried in packs throughout the first year of life learn to walk? But try to tell that to the poor, anxiety-ridden parents who are already addicted to checking the milestone charts to find out whether Junior is crawling and cruising on schedule. Books and programs promoting baby exercise are pandering to parents like these, and only serving to get them more worried. To make matters worse, parents who buy into this approach are setting a dangerous pattern for the future. Let's look at another exercise from the same book to see why.

Turning Over and Back Again
Position: The child flat on his back on a foam rubber mat.

Turning over from flat on the back to flat on the stomach. Cup your right hand under the bent left knee of the child, your wrist keeping the right leg stretched out on the ground . . . Flex his left hip, raise his left buttock, rolling him toward the right side. With the left hand, stretch the child's right arm out and upward . . . Continue turning him over onto his tummy . . . Keep the child interested by patting his bottom or attracting his attention with a toy, and praise him each time he makes an effort. . . .

Aim: Beginnings of a voluntary movement.

What happens when a parent tries to coach a child through a so-called voluntary movement? If the parent tries to take control, is the movement really voluntary? Unfortunately, today's parents seem to find it hard to believe that babies naturally learn to turn over in due time—*without* cradle calisthenics. As time goes by, can we reasonably expect to control every single one of our child's developmental steps this way? Wouldn't it be wiser to begin now to learn that our child is a person in his own right, who will walk and talk according to his own inner timetable?

One reason we're so reluctant to believe that children can develop normally without intensive coaching is that parents often have the milestone charts memorized but have less awareness of the subtleties of how children grow. Unfortunately, when we enroll our kids in franchised movement programs like Gymboree, we are exposed to teachers who often know little more about child development than the average parent. "Many of those places sell franchises, and the franchise owner will hire some auxiliary helpers who have maybe had some experience working with young children, but not in physical settings," says Hammett. Or, on the other hand, they may know more about sports than about young children. No matter how fit an instructor may be or how agile on the uneven parallel bars, unless she has a very clear idea of the young child's emotional and physical development she will not be able to tailor the program to suit this age group.

At an exercise-and-movement class I visited run by Playorena, for example, the teacher sang four different songs to her toddler class in ten minutes—at least three songs more than they could possibly appreciate, let alone participate in, at such a tender age. As one mother, whose child had what appeared to be a slightly palsied arm, proceeded literally to push him to "ride" a ball on his belly and then shove him down the slide as he howled, the instructor said nothing. Eager to sell me on the program, she watched my son crawl into a playhouse of sorts and, rather than offer a word of encouragement or engage him in conversation about what he was doing, began pointing her finger at various pieces of equipment around the room, telling him, "Look, you can go on that, and that, and that!"

Many a parent whose toddler scales the kitchen countertops and escapes from the crib considers kiddie gym a constructive outlet for all that extra energy. But how do early movement or gymnastics classes affect a child's development? Is there any evidence that they produce kids who turn out to be better athletes later on in life?

The more highly structured programs designed as scaled-down versions of instruction methods geared to older children, presenting specific skills, such as traditional gymnastics moves, make even less sense for preschoolers, who have weaker joints, inferior balance, and poorer coordination than their big brothers and sisters. Besides, few are prepared *emotionally* for the stress of being expected to perform or learn specific skills within a structured program. "Children develop at such different rates that unless the program is geared for each child not only physically but emotionally, what happens is that we begin to see children who are afraid of sports," observes Hammett. "They are afraid of physical activity because of the experiences that they have had prior to school age." Saddest of all is the psychological toll on a young child who feels pressured to achieve in a highly structured setting. At a time when healthy self-esteem depends so much on his sense of trust in his parents, he is getting the message that they will love him only as long as he performs. Furthermore, instead of being encouraged to feel comfortable with his body and experience the joy of spontaneous movement, he is learning to depend on adult direction.

Hammett points out that it's highly risky to train toddlers in a particular sport in hope of creating future Olympic stars. "I fear for the children who are talented *more* than for those who are not talented, because the average ones will fall by the wayside," she says. "It's really detrimental to the children who excel because when you hook three-year-olds into gymnastics, and they begin to do nothing but live in that gym, by the time they get to seven or eight—the competitive ages—they have really missed the opportunity to develop *other* physical skills." Unless they can successfully compete at age twelve on the national level, they have sacrificed other kinds of learning, and in many cases an ordinary social life, for the sake of one sport. And with millions of children in this country doing gymnastics and competitive swimming, is it wise focusing your child's interests so narrowly and so early on the infinitesimal chance he'll be the next Kurt Thomas?

Water Play—or Work?

As for infant swimming, you might expect a baby to take to the pool like a duck to water. Somehow, though, when infants are formally taught to swim, it turns into highly serious business. Where's the warmth or humor in a book like Claire Timmermans's (1976) *How to Teach Your Baby to Swim?* "Constant practice is absolutely essential," she warns. "Babies who float quite happily at five or six months can become interested in their toes when eight months of age. As it is impossible for a baby to float when his hands are clutching his feet, it is essential that a good floating habit be established before eight months of age."

And listen to the no-nonsense treatment recommended by authors Whitehead and Curtis in *How to Watersafe Infants and Toddlers:*

> When your child's hair is dirty, you let him know he must have his hair washed. He knows nothing will change your mind—even crying won't help. If your child is like this, you have already learned the secret of *firm expectations.*
>
> At certain points in your child's water-safety training, you are going to have to "wash his hair." You must make progress, and he must learn.
>
> Let your child know you have firm expectations. No amount of crying will make you take him out of the water.

The purpose of this boot-camp approach? To make sure your child learns to *save himself from drowning* the next time he takes a surprise belly flop into your backyard pool. Ironically, as many experts point out, the net result of an infant swimming program may well be a child who is *less safe* around water because he feels no compunction about stepping off the edge of the pool at the drop of a hat, and because his mother has been lulled into believing that if he does he'll "pop up to the surface like a little cork," as one author puts it. A dangerous sort of confidence develops.

But no one—adult or child—is ever "truly drownproofed," according to Millard Freeman, national director of aquatics for the YMCA of the USA.

Do infants who take Water Babies classes end up better swimmers? Most studies show that normal children's physical development proceeds in a defined *sequence.* Open a book on the motor development of young children and you'll find charts and photographs of the stages of early walking and manipulation, for example. An infant actually *begins* to learn to walk as early as three months. So invariable is this *sequence* in the healthy infant that pediatricians use it as a diagnostic tool, testing everything from the newborn's reflexive crawling to the preschooler's walking down a flight of stairs using an alternate foot pattern. Likewise, the development of swimming movements has been found to follow a predictable sequence, from the newborn's swimming reflex to the preschooler's leg-dominated stroke (at around age three and one-half) to an overarm stroke. But child-development specialists agree that although this *sequence* of changes remains essentially the same from child to child, the *rate* of development varies. In other words (as most parents know) children tend to develop along the same lines, but some of them do so faster than others. The big question is, which is the key determining factor—the child's genetically determined *maturity* or influences in his *environment?*

One study frequently trotted out as an answer to this question was done in 1935 by Dr. Myrtle McGraw of Columbia University and Babies Hospital, who experimented with twins known as Johnny and Jimmy. During their first seventeen months of life Johnny received weekly water training, while Jimmy did not. At age six Johnny swam in a horizontal position using a well-coordinated front crawl pattern, but his brother swam in a vertical dog-paddle. Jimmy caught up on his swimming skills, but Johnny retained a self-confidence, an ease and grace of movement, that persisted in later life.

Unfortunately, since this study failed to include systematic observation of the twins during their preschool years, its results can't be considered a clear indication that the first seventeen months were the critical ones. Books promoting infant swimming instruction that cite this study as evidence of its effectiveness, therefore, are basing their claims on incomplete data.

In Benjamin Bloom's study of the development of Olympic swimmers, reported in *Developing Talent in Young People,* not one champion counts having been dunked as a newborn among his formative childhood experiences. One young man, Peter, recalls having been introduced to the water and to swimming by his mother, who taught him the basics in a low-key way one summer when he was six years old. That winter she took him and his brother to a community center with a swimming program, but Peter did not really have the opportunity to swim on a regular basis until he was nine and his family moved to the East Coast. Their new home happened to be near a large lake where everyone in the town went swimming, and Peter and his brother spent the long summer days there. Swimming was something they did for fun.

Ask Millard Freeman of the YMCA whether a kid's lost his shot at a gold medal if he misses out on infant swimming, and Freeman quickly denies it. In fact, he says, *"eight* seems to be a darn good age. The child who starts at eight has no fear and catches up quickly with the child who started at two, three, or four."

Others agree. "There is little justification for infant 'swimming' or water adjustment programs," declared the American Academy of Pediatrics in a 1985 policy statement. "It is unlikely that infants can be made 'water safe'; in fact, the parents of these infants may develop a false sense of security if they believe that their infant can 'swim' a few strokes." Ultimately, the only way you can "watersafe" your child is by keeping an eye on him. You don't expect him to fix his own dinner, or go for a walk on the street alone: why do so many parents accept the idea that infants and toddlers can act as their own lifeguards in the pool? "We counted to three and blew in their faces, which made them hold their breath," recalled one mother who pulled her child out of a "watersafing" program. "But my goal was just to have him feel comfortable in the water. I'm the parent—ultimately it's *my* responsibility to keep my child from drowning."

And there are other dangers as well. Unless the infant swimming program takes place at home in your bathtub (an approach which is in fact recommended in several books), your child is definitely at higher risk of exposure to infectious disease by being in a pool with other babies. In its position paper the AAP clearly states that certain disease bacteria are transmitted through feces in the water and warns that precautions should be taken to contain the problem—literally. This is quite a contrast to Danuta Rylko's recommendation in *Watersafe Your Baby in One Week* (1983) that "bathing-suits, rubber pants, and diapers will only hinder the baby's movement. . . . To make learning as easy as possible, dump the diapers! (In case there's little 'accident' in the pool, the filter will do its job, and the chlorine will come to the rescue. What floats can be scooped out.)" There is also the threat of "water intoxication"—disorientation and vomiting when the baby swallows too much water.

As of now, there's no real evidence that kiddie swim classes are going to turn your child into a future gold medalist. If you enjoy holding your baby in the water and he seems to be having fun, then enjoy yourselves together. In the long run, keep in mind that having fun in the water during these early years may be the most important factor in motivating your child to develop his swimming abilities.

Healthy Ways to Help

Does this mean that any attempt to encourage a young child's physical development is a waste of time, or that there is absolutely no place for young children's water or gym programs? Not in the least. Previous generations of kids may have developed their coordination, balance, and agility on the playground, or playing kickball in the street, or climbing fences, but many of today's kids lack these opportunities. In our concern to keep our children safe from harm, we allow them less freedom to roam through neighborhoods and fields than we ourselves had as children. According to a recent study done in New York City, children in high-rise buildings are not allowed to play outside alone until they reach an average age of *ten*. Children of working parents who spend the day in child-care centers often have limited space and equipment, and in many centers physical education is often not a priority.

Ironically, one of the biggest obstacles to children's exercise is the superbaby syndrome itself. Children who are kept occupied in preschools and at home with workbooks and ditto sheets are missing out on desperately needed hours of running, jumping, and ball-playing. "The problem in today's society is that we think computers are better for children than bats and balls," Carol Hammett says bluntly. Many preschool directors, scrambling to meet the demand for highly academic programs, fail to incorporate physical development as an essential part of their programs. I visited one school where outdoor space was cramped and the playground equipment was a single climbing frame. "Is physical activity an important part of your program?" I inquired. "Oh, yes, we make sure the children—especially the *boys*—get out at least once a day to blow off some steam," answered the director impatiently.

That kind of attitude reflects a belief that physical development is less important than other aspects of growth, a view that shows little understanding of the young child. Early-childhood specialists repeatedly caution that cognitive learning is inexorably tied in with physical development. It is only through acquiring a healthy sense of his body and its relation to the world around him that your preschooler becomes prepared for abstract functions such as reading and mathematics. As he crawls *through* a play tunnel or climbs *under* a bar of the jungle gym, he is getting a much more vivid understanding of prepositions than he ever could from a workbook, for example.

So where do you start? Rather than focusing on the acquisition of specific skills—like performing on the parallel bars or learning the crawl stroke—Carol Hammett recommends that a young child's physical education be designed to introduce him to a *variety of basic movements.* Although specific skills learned in well-conceived programs may play a part, you can also help your child find simple ways to gain physical confidence and coordination in the course of a normal day's activities. First of all, consider what your child *already* does in the course of a day. If he spends most of his time at home, is there space for running, jumping, hopping, skipping, and other locomotor skills? Does he play ball with you, his siblings, a regular baby-sitter, or the neighborhood kids? Do you have access to a place to enjoy water play—the YMCA, perhaps, or even a large inflatable pool? Is there a park with a playground nearby? Are there other kids in the neighborhood to inspire him to try shooting baskets, say, or tip-toeing along the curb (the original balance beam)? Are riding toys available? Do you or a care-giver play games like "red light, green light," or sing songs with gestures or fingerplays?

If he attends a day-care center or preschool, find out exactly what part movement plays in the program: what kinds of space and equipment are available, how much time is set aside for physical education, whether the teachers foster kids' awareness of movement through dance, musical activities, or age-appropriate games?

If, after an analysis of your child's day, you still feel he needs an outside program—because of space limitations, perhaps, or a scarcity of neighborhood kids—the key is to find one that is *developmentally appropriate,* both physically and emotionally, for a toddler or preschooler. There are movement programs offered by commercial enterprises such as Gymboree, as well as boys' clubs, the YMCA, and community recreation programs. These tend to emphasize free play on a variety of equipment, with movement to music. By contrast, gymnastics clubs tend to use more conventional gymnastics apparatus and may emphasize training in specific movements and gymnastic skills. Also, you may find a water-adjustment class at the Y and virtually anyplace else that has a pool. No matter where it's given, don't assume a program is good without watching a class, using one of the checklists below.

Gymnastics or Movement Program Checklist

☐ Is there "open viewing," that is, are parents welcome to visit sessions at any time? For children younger than two and one-half, a parent or care-giver should be an active participant, "spotting" the child for safety, offering encouragement, praise, and reassurance.

☐ What are the qualifications of the owner and the teachers, as well as the director? They should be experts in physical education, but that's not enough. "The problem is, you may have a PE teacher who's taught twenty years at the high school level," points out Carol Hammett. "The physical educator and the staff need to be trained in early-childhood development, so they know how to teach *children,* not just teach gymnastics or dance."

☐ Is the program safe? If children are climbing, or up off the ground, there should be adequate padding. "In our facility, as a rule of thumb, they are not allowed to climb on anything higher than their head unless there's an eight-inch crash mat underneath and a teacher spotting them," says Hammett. "Even the most coordinated children break bones."

☐ Is the equipment in good repair? Is it suited to a young child's size and strength? Keep in mind that although many facilities offer trampolines, the American Academy of Pediatrics has published a position statement cautioning that trampolines have caused a "high number of quadriplegic injuries"; that even for schoolchildren they "should not be a part of routine physical education classes"; and that the trampoline "should *never* be used in home or recreational settings. . . ."

☐ Is a child freely allowed to choose *not* to do a particular activity? If he is afraid to crawl across the bars, he should be able to say so without fear of disapproval or coercion. "There has to be a trust between the teacher and the child, and between the parent and the child, and it has to be earned," says Gordon Shaw, former president and now treasurer of the U.S. Association of Independent Gymnastics Clubs and the owner of Virginia's Richmond Olympiad.

☐ Does the director or instructor make an effort to educate parents? "What we try to do in our setting is make sure the parents focus on their own child as an individual," says Hammett. "The teacher's responsibility is to let the parents know, time and time again—and it's included in the daily discussion—that children develop at different rates, and if parents get pushy the children will just retaliate by not doing the activity. And I think it's the teacher's responsibility to have a serious discussion with pushy parents."

Water or Swimming Program Checklist

■ Does the program conform to the American Academy of Pediatrics guidelines on infant swimming programs? These include

Prohibiting "dunking."

Keeping the water temperature at eighty-three to eighty-six degrees Fahrenheit to prevent chills.

Providing measures to control fecal contamination.

Having each infant on a one-on-one basis with a parent or responsible adult. "Organized group swimming instruction should be reserved for children more than three years of age." The instructor isn't teaching your baby, but giving you suggestions on how to help your child enjoy the water.

☐ Are the instructors qualified to *teach* (not just Red Cross-certified lifeguards) and familiar with infant CPR techniques?

☐ Is the pool properly maintained and the water kept clean?

☐ Are infants with known medical problems required to receive their physician's approval before participating?

☐ Do the kids seem happy? "If there's an inordinate amount of crying among the children, I'd want to know why," says Millard Freeman of the YMCA. "That's their way of saying, 'I don't like this.'" At first young children usually *are* scared, says Freeman: "What we find is that kids associate water with soap in their eyes, so they come to associate water with hurt and burning." Soon enough, though, they should be having fun.

☐ Are children encouraged to wear safe flotation devices? These should be cubes attached by means of a belt or vest—not loose rings or tubes—so that kids can concentrate on movement in the water. "Gradually," says Freeman, "they can go from two cubes to one, then use a kickboard at around age two."

☐ Does the instructor view the class as an opportunity for children to get comfortable in the water, or as an early start on Olympic training? Is the class seen as a chance for parents to be educated about *real* water safety? Steer clear of courses that promise to "watersafe" or "drownproof" your child.

☐ Does the teacher give instructions in advance to parents about potential dangers? The signs of water intoxication in a child,

for example—disorientation, vomiting, and irritability—
should send you immediately to the emergency room. To
prevent drowning, a life preserver should be available, and
even if a child who has been accidentally submerged seems
fine, he should be taken to the emergency room to be
checked for water in the lungs.

☐ Consider how prepared *you* are to help your child enjoy the
water in a pressure-free way. "We have parents who push
children too soon," says Freeman. "My major problem is
not with the children, it's with the parents. There's no question that there are a lot of fathers who say, 'My boy's gonna
do this like I did.' They completely turn the kids off."

If you decide to introduce your child to organized classes in
swimming or movement, keep in mind that the emotional style
of your approach will make the difference between turning him
on or off. The point is not to pressure him to achieve, but to keep
it *fun*. And if you're *not* inclined to enroll him, there's certainly
no reason to feel apologetic. Kids have been getting exercise and
learning to feel comfortable in the water at playgrounds and in
backyard kiddie pools for a long time. Whether he's in a class or
an informal situation, there's no reliable evidence to show that
teaching *specific skills* at this stage will necessarily produce a better
athlete, but your child will gain confidence and a positive attitude
toward his body. As always, just relax and enjoy your time together.

Computers for Preschoolers: Indispensable Teacher or Expensive Toy?

"I don't know anything about computers myself, but I'm told that they're the thing now. Your life is so affected by the computer world that if you're not in it, you're going to be lost."

—Mother of a three-year-old boy

Why not help your youngster get a start on the computer age? What scientists once thought would always be multimillion-dollar machines tucked away in research laboratories can now be purchased for the price of a color television set. Better yet is that children can become adept in the use of the machines in just a few weeks.

—Frederick and Victoria Williams, *Growing Up With Computers,* 1983

Albert the Teaching Robot Teaches Your Child to Read & Do Math: Give your 3–6-year-old a head start! Albert responds to correct answers with space-age Light and Sound!

—Magazine advertisement

WE'RE HARDLY THE FIRST generation to marvel at kids' easy familiarity with subject matter that boggles the mind of many an adult. As far back as 1907, *Playthings* magazine was similarly dazzled by the possibilities for kids who had wind-up or friction-powered toy cars or trucks to play with: "The mechanical toys of the time cannot come into a boy's possession without giving him a certain acquisition of mechanical ideas which may be valuable to him in his future career. The 20th century boy of ten years is in a fair way to know more about the possibilities of electricity than the professor of natural philosophy understood fifty years ago."

Today, for the average adult computer illiterate, the mere sight of a child sitting at an electronic keyboard is proof that he or she is a veritable computer genius. And so, we're easy marks. Like the fast-talking encyclopedia salesmen of the post-World War II era, who sold their product by telling our parents we'd flunk out of school without it, the manufacturers of kids' computers and computer toys know exactly how to strike fear into the hearts of today's parents. They name their products Little Genius and Dial-A-Teacher. They promise miracles of learning, from number and letter recognition to shapes and colors. There's even software aimed at capturing the two-and-a-half-year-old market! Imagine an electronic toy that looks like a television set, is as much fun as a video game, and teaches everything, from reading to geometry to chess. Sounds like every parent and child's dream machine. Unless you know your way around a computer yourself, it's hard to know what's hype and what isn't.

Most of the experts quoted in the popular press have done little more than confound the issue. In one corner we have those who claim young children weaned on computers will usher in a new golden age of brilliance. On the other side are the skeptics who say, among other, less kind things, that education by computer is bound to create a culture of psychopaths.

Virtually everyone does agree, however, that computers are here to stay. As our children grow to adulthood in the electronic age, the critical issue is not *whether* they will use computers, but *how.* As we shall see, each side in the controversy takes a different perspective on the computer's potential role in the learning process.

The Computer as Pencil and Other Bright Ideas

Not only the computer industry but many educators see computers as powerful learning tools for even the youngest children. Probably the most influential is Seymour Papert, an MIT mathematician and disciple of Piaget who invented LOGO, a programming language for children. In his book *Mindstorms* (1980) Papert explains the process of learning math through programming by recalling his own childhood fascination with automobile gears. "The gear can be used to illustrate many powerful 'advanced' mathematical ideas, such as groups or relative motion," he writes. "But it does more than this. As well as connecting with the formal knowledge of mathematics, it also connects with the 'body knowledge,' the sensorimotor schemata of a child. You can *be* the gear, you can understand how it turns by projecting yourself into its place and turning with it."

Likewise, in Papert's vision, children who work in LOGO learn to move a "turtle" (really a triangle) around the screen, projecting themselves into its place and turning with it. LOGO offers the preschooler the opportunity to use the "computer as pencil," in Papert's phrase—to decide what she wants to do and how she will go about it, just as she would with building blocks or Play-Doh. What better way for a child to get used to symbolic or abstract thinking?

Because they become deeply absorbed in making the turtle move, and because they're having fun doing it, Papert reasons, children will not only develop the ability to think mathematically, but will come to love math. "I remember that there was *feeling, love,* as well as understanding in my relationship with gears," he writes. His goal in designing LOGO was to take advantage of the computer's ability to simulate and "turn computers into instruments flexible enough so that many children can each create for themselves something like what the gears were for me."

Ideally, this approach to learning is exactly the opposite of the one taken by America's most popular electronic toy—television. " 'Sesame Street' might offer better and more engaging explanations than a child can get from some parents or nursery-school teachers, but the child is still in the position of listening to explanations," Papert observes. "By contrast, when a child learns to program, the process of learning is transformed. It becomes more active and self-directed."

Learning through LOGO is also intended to be more active than "traditional" computer instruction—the software packages marketed to schools and parents, usually sold through computer dealers and large toy stores. With these traditional instructional packages, the computer programs the child by providing structured exercises and offering feedback. But with LOGO the child is in the driver's seat.

However, many computer boosters have good things to say about ordinary commercial software for preschoolers, too. They claim that the computer is a teaching tool that is interactive, versatile, and fun, and that even run-of-the-mill programs have an appeal that is unique in several ways:

- Educators point out that good programs for three-, four-, and five-year-olds are designed to be both fun and accessible to kids who have not yet learned to read. Through color, graphics, and musical tones they offer a child the opportunity to play independent games, "draw" on the screen, and answer questions.

- Obviously, they promote computer literacy by giving kids hands-on experience at a tender age.

- By replacing text with graphics, and limiting use of the keyboard to only a few keys (or bypassing it in favor of a joystick or mouse, with voice commands in the not-too-distant future), they give three- and four-year-olds a feeling of competence and even power. "A good piece of software can allow youngsters to master tasks that might be hard in the more complex real world," comments Charles Hohmann, Ph.D., manager of the computers and young children program at the High/Scope Educational Research Foundation. The child who's having a tough time building a drivable road out of blocks for his toy trucks, for example, may find it easier to "make" one on the computer.

■ An uncluttered screen with one flashing shape or image can be easier to focus on than a board game with lots of pieces. (And parents, incidentally, like the fact that there are no cards or dice to get lost or damaged.)

■ Computers, even with educational programs, can be as much fun as video games. ("Let's play the game that shoots at the numbers!" my son begged on a recent trip to our public library's computer corner.)

■ Many preschool software programs can be adapted to suit your child's developmental stage—you can make the alphabet fly by at faster or slower rates, or vary the rate at which numerals are breathed by a dragon.

■ There are programs to suit nearly every taste. With assorted "bells and whistles," a child can draw pictures on the screen (using a "paint," or graphics, program) or write her own songs (with a music synthesizer). And, of course, there's always the shoot-em-up that lets her fire away at shapes, numbers, or letters.

■ Despite widespread concern that computers will create a generation of nursery-school "nerds"—whiz kids at math but washouts on the playground—many observers have noted that computers actually seem to *encourage* social interaction among children. Researchers at the University of Minnesota Institute of Education, for example, compared children working with a computer with others doing picture puzzles, and found that the kids were much more likely to work in teams at the computer than on the puzzles.

An Apple in the Garden of Eden?

A 'pre-computer' for ages 3–5. . . . Helps children learn colors and shapes, numbers and letters, counting, spelling, music and more!
—*Dial-A-Teacher package copy*

The idea of a young child—knees scraped, pockets gritty with sand from the sandbox, head filled with a hodgepodge of fear, misunderstanding, and wonder—staring transfixed at a computer screen rubs a lot of people the wrong way. Like television, a computer doesn't offer the child a chance to touch, smell, or feel what's on the screen; it's strictly two-dimensional.

No matter how user-friendly the software, there's nothing personal about an electronic box. And, say the critics, every minute spent at the keyboard robs a child of her once-in-a-lifetime chance to taste honeysuckle, make mudpies, and (yes!) smell the roses.

One of the strongest fears voiced by many educators is that children who grow up with computers will never really learn how to get along with others. Instead of sitting together in the preschool classroom at a child-size table, talking and making collages from a shared pile of materials, "computer kids" sit in isolation staring at a screen that offers no human interaction. One group of researchers has even suggested that having kids work at computers is a threat to world peace, because it deprives them of the opportunity to develop concern for others!

Two professors at California State University at Fullerton, B.J. Barnes and Shirley Hill, touched a nerve in the educational community when they published an article entitled "Should Young Children Work with Microcomputers—LOGO Before Lego?" In Piagetian terms, they recommend waiting until a child has reached the stage of concrete operations, around age seven, before starting her off at the computer. By this time, they explain, the child can reason logically and understand that objects have such properties as volume and number. By contrast, the "preoperational" child, dominated by her perceptions of the moment, needs to practice physical skills and get hands-on experience of the real world.

"The child who is building with blocks learns basic physical principles when a poorly balanced tower crashes to the floor," note Barnes and Hill. "The child stacking pots and pans in the kitchen learns about graduated sizes. The child who kicks another and gets kicked in return quickly learns that kicking hurts. These learnings, so essential to functioning in the world, may not be replicated with a keyboard and CRT [cathode-ray tube, or computer screen]."

Experimenting with three-dimensional materials is a matchless opportunity for open-ended exploration. When your child does something as simple as pouring sand from one pail to another, for example, she begins to understand the concept of volume. Most preschool software programs, on the other hand, are rigidly designed to elicit one right answer, and often an adult is needed to read the instructions. Barnes and Hill point out that LOGO does make it possible for kids to experiment, but only once they've cottoned on to a complex set of commands to move the turtle. (In fact, many preschools doctor the program to create a simple-to-use, one-key or "instant" version of LOGO.) Furthermore, they note drily, just as Papert recalls how his own love of gears helped *him* learn to think, today's young children benefit from contact with real objects, too.

"This is not to say that a preoperational child would be harmed by contact with a computer," the researchers are quick to add. "However, experiences with a computer should never replace their experiences with real events and objects." After all, there are only so many hours in a day. "Children at microcomputers are not using all the senses so essential to understanding the world in which they will be living. They are being limited to dealing with two-dimensional abstractions of real objects that are represented on a screen."

Obviously, the average preschooler who watches some twenty-five hours of television a week risks further deprivation—not to mention eyestrain and fatigue—by being planted in front of a computer.

Other critics say that most educational programs amount to little more than electronic flashcards. Even worse, they are likely to turn kids off by trying to teach concepts—such as left and right, up and down—which would be far more effectively learned through physical movement. Some educators worry that kids who grow up with computers will come to expect all learning to feature number-shooting and the alphabet on parade. In his book *Insult to Intelligence,* Frank Smith warns: "The underlying implication of 'learning should be fun' is that learning *will be* a painful and tedious activity unless it is primped up as entertainment."

The critics also scoff at the argument that early computer literacy is *de rigueur* for the twenty-first-century child. Although our kids are very likely to be using computers on the job and even at home, they don't necessarily need to start when they're still in diapers. After all, as Charles Hohmann of the High/Scope Educational Research Foundation points out, *"We* didn't have computers at home because they didn't exist. And we're making it!" Besides, most of what your child learns about computers today is going to be obsolete by the time she lands her first job, somewhere around 2010, because new hardware and software technology is being developed at a ferocious rate. Finally, most of our kids are going to be computer *users*—in business and law offices, banks, airline terminals, and hospitals—not programmers. As such, they will need to acquire enough knowledge, skill, and judgment *in their chosen careers* to be able to evaluate the data stored on their computers, but they won't need to understand a great deal about hardware and software. As one critic asks, "How many drivers understand the theory of the internal combustion engine?" On the road, it's driving skill and experience that count. Likewise, your child's capacity to find her way in the ever-changing adult world will depend on such broad factors as reasoning, critical thinking, ability to learn from experience, interpersonal skills, and motivation—not on specific technical knowledge.

So Many Claims, So Few Facts

Which side is right? Does the computer unleash a child's hidden learning potential—or stifle it?

Unfortunately for our generation of parents, there isn't much long-term research available, since home computers have been popular for little more than ten years as of this writing. As Shirley Hill and Elizabeth Brady note in an article published in *Young Children,* even the so-called scientific studies are astonishingly inadequate. "When reviewing the current research relating to young children and computers, it becomes clear that there is much more rhetoric than solid evidence, that current studies have used very small groups, have maintained few standard research controls, and usually involve a university setting and population . . ."

Few studies have focused on children under the age of eight. Even Papert has been repeatedly criticized for offering anecdotal accounts of kids' use of LOGO, rather than controlled studies. Other researchers have sought to fill the gap; one study, reported in 1983, found that young children learned little from LOGO, although it did benefit third-graders. Another study of fourteen preschoolers using the program over an eight-month period revealed that, despite Papert's claim that all children could learn from it, only certain kids seem to function well with LOGO. Those who did, interestingly enough, were not found to be brighter in math or more creative, but merely more experienced with computers and arcade games in and out of their homes.

And even within the research available, there is a puzzling conflict. A study designed to determine whether computers help kindergartners learn to count and to recognize shapes found no significant differences between the control and experimental groups. Yet another group of researchers, writing in 1982, concluded that computer games enhanced the development of primary-school children's understanding of basic math.

Another point of contention is the relationship between computer use and gender among young children. Some have suggested that early introduction of computers will prevent sex-stereotyping, that little girls will take to them as enthusiastically as little boys and therefore grow up ready to enter high-paying technical fields, just like boys. Researchers at the University of Minnesota Institute of Education found that, unlike school-age girls, who are less likely to decide to work on computers than their male counterparts, preschool girls and boys are equally interested in computers. As a result, some have suggested that it makes sense to introduce computers to four-year-olds in an effort to close the gender gap. But a 1983 study at Ball State University found that even preschool boys chose to use the computer (instead of four other typical nursery school activities) significantly *more often* than girls. And yet another study reported in the same year found that preschool boys preferred LOGO-type, open-ended programs, while girls favored drill-and-practice software. At first glance, this seems like bad news for girls, but could it in fact reflect *strengths* typically attributed to them by early-childhood specialists, mothers, and nursery school teachers? Girls are often described as more social, for example; perhaps they prefer to play dress-up together with friends, rather than sit at a computer alone. (Would they be more inclined to use the computer in small groups?) Girls are also typically ahead of boys in reading-readiness skills; could it be that they are attracted to drill-and-practice programs more often than boys because they are rewarded with more right answers? We need to know more, but it seems fair to conclude that early computer training per se is not likely to make boys and girls think or develop alike, and that instructors need to pay attention to gender-associated differences in learning styles and tailor their programs appropriately. If those of us who are parents of girls keep this in mind, we will not be deluded into thinking early computer use is a yellow brick road to sexual equality for our daughters.

Finally, no one can really predict the physical effects of long-term computer use starting in early childhood. Scientific research has focused on adults who sit at the screen for much of the workday. Studies of clerical workers using computers (summarized in a 1981 National Institute for Occupational Safety and Health report) found symptoms of psychological distress, including anxiety, depression, irritability, fatigue, and lack of inner security. And many adult computer users complain of eyestrain and back stress after long hours at the screen. Finally, there have been many reports of unexplained clusters of problem pregnancies (miscarriages and birth defects) among workers in computerized offices. The long-term effects on today's children, who are the first generation with lifelong exposure to computers, have yet to be studied. In the meantime, we owe it to our kids to watch for symptoms of psychological stress, to listen for complaints of physical strain, and to be sure they are using the safest possible computer setup (See the next section).

Healthy Ways to Help

With computers already ensconced in hospitals, banks, hotels, the travel industry, and schools, common sense tells you preschoolers ought to have *some* contact with them, just as they do with fire engines, dolls, and books. "I think that kids learn from a lot of different experiences," says High/Scope's Charles Hohmann. "Computers are just one more way kids can work with concepts and ideas that they can control."

Most computer experts think it's important for today's generation to grow up feeling comfortable with computers, not awed by them, and understanding both the machine's potential and its limitations. How to accomplish this?

1. Make sure you're not overwhelmed by computers yourself. Let's say you think of computers as mysterious electronic brains that threaten someday to go haywire and take over the world—or at least run up bills on everyone's charge accounts. Unless you've got hands-on computer experience yourself, you're at the mercy of what you see in the movies and advertisements. How can you possibly offer your preschooler a realistic perspective? And if you exhibit a nervous tic, or shrug your shoulders every time you hear the word *computer,* you're setting your preschooler up to be intimidated or, worse, to believe that computers have power over us—not that we control computers.

The best way to combat this attitude is to remember that a computer can't do anything at all unless a human being programs it. Every time the phone company or the bank tells you, "It was a computer error," realize that *there's no such thing.* Errors are made by *people* who program computers and supply them with information. For this reason, computer experts have a popular saying: "Garbage in, garbage out." If a person feeds a computer incorrect data, the computer will spew forth mistakes.

Beyond a change in your way of thinking about computers, you may find it helpful to try using one in a relaxed fashion over a period of weeks. Hands-on experience with a few educational programs will quickly make it clear that there's nothing to be nervous about. If you can use the automatic teller machine at the bank, you can use the computer. *Don't* be put off by previous experiences with bad programs; computer software has come a long way in terms of user-friendliness since you were in college. And if you've written off computers as a result of attending a poorly taught class on the subject, try sitting down at a keyboard with a computer-literate friend at the public library, your office, or a computer dealer. As with everything, from snorkeling to lovemaking, the best way to understand what it's like is to try it for yourself.

2. Help your child to understand how computers are used in the context of her daily life. Barbara Bowman, director of graduate studies at Chicago's Erikson Institute and a researcher on preschoolers' use of computers, offers little encouragement for parents who hope the computer will turn their preschoolers into budding geniuses. "My purpose would not be to *teach* the child something with the computer. What you want him to learn is that computers are fun," she says. "I sure wouldn't go out and buy a computer for a three-year-old, but I wouldn't hesitate to go out and buy one for a five-year-old."

Bowman recommends a low-key approach she likens to the development of print awareness: "Kids learn that books have interesting information in them, that books are useful. They don't learn about print in an organized way, the way an adult would learn a foreign language; they build an overview of the whole process."

You can help your child build this overview even if you fail to provide her with her own personal computer as soon as she outgrows her Cradle Gym. When you're visiting the bank or the supermarket together, point out the computers in operation. You might offer a simple explanation of how and why the computer is used in a particular situation ("to tell us how much money we have to pay for our food," and so on).

At home, let her loose on an old typewriter to help her get accustomed to the QWERTY keyboard and the use of the shift key and space bar, which she'll encounter later on at the computer. (But don't *worry* if you haven't got an old typewriter.)

If you already have a home computer, Bowman suggests, let your child see you using it, and give her a chance to play at it just as she would turn the pages of a book.

Should you decide to offer your child the opportunity for hands-on experience with a computer (either at home or at the public library), be sure to introduce her to it in a way that makes sense, just as you'd present a new book. Otherwise, says High/Scope's Charles Hohmann, she is likely to sit in front of the screen wondering, What am I supposed to do? What is this thing about? What's the game here?

According to Dr. Hohmann, one of the most successful ways to introduce a new software program is by focusing first on the activity or concept it features—before you even turn on the computer. Let's say, for example, your child is about to try "Estimation," a program that involves learning to start and stop a little train on the screen in order to explore concepts of time. At the High/Scope Demonstration Preschool, the first thing the teachers do when introducing this program is to take out a three-dimensional wooden train and have the children practice starting and stopping it on top of the table. Only then do the kids get a chance to try it on the screen. "You want to strengthen the link between what children might be doing on the computer and other parts of their experience," says Dr. Hohmann.

Once your child feels comfortable with a program, she will enjoy using it independently. Yet just as you try to be responsive to your child's block-building and fantasies, says Dr. Hohmann, it's helpful to participate in her computer time—offering help when she needs it, and asking probing questions that will stimulate her thinking.

3. *Focus on what your child can do, not what the computer can do.* Like a TV set, the computer screen can be mesmerizing. It's easy to get so wrapped up in the leaping letters and flying numbers on the screen that you forget who's supposed to be running the show—your child, not the machine. No matter how exciting the software, if it doesn't suit your child's level of cognitive development or personal preferences, it's not worth the diskette it's copied on.

Before a child can understand the meaning of symbols on the screen, she needs plenty of experience with three-dimensional objects in the real world. "You hear claims like, 'A mouse with a Macintosh—a three-year-old can do it,'" says Marge Kosel, vice president of Sunburst Communications, a major producer of educational software. "But I think moving something down here [on the keyboard] and having something happen up there [on the screen] is hard for a young child. It all depends on the child's stage of development. But there's no reason to believe that the majority of three-year-olds are ready for it."

It's also important to consider your preschooler's daily habits before setting her up at a computer: Is she already spending hours a day in front of a television screen? In that case, extra time at a monitor might be better spent collecting leaves outdoors, or playing dress-up.

Finally, no matter how much she enjoys the computer, realize that there will be days when she's just not in the mood. "There are times when we come and he's not interested, so we just do something else," said the mother of a four-year-old who visits her local public library every week for a session at the computer. "Or if there are a lot of kids here, he's more interested in being with them than sitting at the keyboard. That's fine—there's always next time."

4. *Help keep it fun by not imposing your grown-up goal orientation and lengthy attention span.* The first time I sat down at a computer with my son, it seemed to me we'd barely turned on the machine when he said, "I don't want to do it any more," and trotted off to do a puzzle. Checking my watch, I was amazed to discover we'd been at it for fifteen minutes—quite a while for a three-year-old to put up with a ho-hum drill-and-practice program. The next time, I found software with jazzier graphics and better games, and I ended up having to all but drag him away after forty minutes.

According to an informal study reported in *Key Notes* (The High/Scope Early Childhood Computer Learning Report), preschool children average twelve minutes per computer session. Not to worry, says the report, this is long enough to play a whole game or complete a drawing.

Even if games and drawings go unfinished, though, remember that your goals are to help your child become familiar with the computer, to help her enjoy it, and to let her realize that people control computers, not vice versa. You're defeating the last two purposes if you try to force her to finish a game or activity after she's lost interest.

5. *Choose age-appropriate software.* The best preschool software features picture menus from which the child can select the activity or game of her choice, rather than a sea of directions that must

be read by an adult. "Look for a clean screen," recommends Marge Kosel of Sunburst Communications. "Some of them have writing all over them. They should be just like storybooks, with pictures the child can recognize and connect with—just as, after you've read him a story over and over, he can 'read' it back to you by looking at the pictures."

You may be able to preview programs at your computer store or public library. (A few manufacturers also offer a refund on returned programs within thirty days.) Children's software can be divided into two main categories: the *highly structured* programs (computer games and drill-and-practice) and *open-ended* programs (simulations and LOGO).

Despite advertisers' claims to the contrary, drill and practice doesn't really *teach* kids to read or do math. It just gives them a chance to practice what they've already learned. A capital letter might be shown on the screen, and your child required to hit a key every time its lowercase counterpart appears. Unless she already has some familiarity with the alphabet, she won't be able to do the drill.

The style is often shoot-em-up, along the lines of a video or arcade game, although some programs feature popular characters like the Peanuts gang and the "Sesame Street" Muppets.

Many kids find drill-and-practice programs more fun than workbooks, although they're certainly no more creative. Look for programs that offer lots of positive feedback for correct answers. (I previewed a few that rewarded every wrong answer with an on-screen explosion, while a correct response triggered nothing more thrilling than proceeding to the next question.) Also check the user's manual to see whether the program can be adapted (faster or slower questions, easier or more challenging drills) to your child's level.

The main drawback to drill-and-practice programs is their emphasis on right and wrong answers. Unfortunately, they dominate the preschool market, creating the impression among some parents (and, worse, kids) that if Justin or Sarah isn't proficient at number or letter recognition, computers are over his or her head.

Nevertheless, young children often find games that call for a right answer very satisfying, particularly if they succeed in getting the right answer often. "I don't think it's doing a youngster a lot of harm," says Charles Hohmann. "I would hope that's not the only thing they're doing." On the other hand, the unstructured approach offered with many "paint" (graphics) or word-processing programs is too freewheeling for many preschoolers. "What are appropriate are the programs that provide a *degree* of open-endedness in their exploration. They provide *some* structure, so that the child can define the task that he or she will undertake and then have some room to be nominally creative in that context." Unfortunately, says Hohmann, such programs are few and far between.

Fortunately, however, a few *simulations* for preschoolers are beginning to come on the market. These offer a child the opportunity to use her imagination by finding her way through a variety of situations at the computer. She might pretend to be a window washer and select which windows to wash, for example, as in the Fisher-Price Memory Manor program. Likewise a paint or graphics program is an opportunity to foster creativity. It gives her a chance to use the computer as a crayon, which can be fun if she manages to make the cognitive leap required to understand that hitting a key makes a line move on the screen.

No matter what type of program you select, pay attention to the quality of the graphics: many are so bad that a child who recognizes typeset letters and numerals may be baffled by the primitive clusters of dots on the screen. This is good preparation for using computers, no doubt, but hardly encouraging for the prereader or budding mathematician!

Programs that use voice simulation (a voice speaking along with the action on the screen) are often a problem. In many cases, the voice is unclear to the point of being incomprehensible. "We've avoided putting anything out with a voice because we feel there isn't anything high enough in quality yet. We feel it would confuse children as much as help them. But the market is almost forcing us into it," says Sunburst's Kosel. "It's very hard to get high quality within the confines of what the average customer will pay."

Many of the programs currently on the market treat the same subject matter—the numbers and the good old ABCs. If you plan to acquire several programs, aim for some diversity—games, graphics, and music, for example. Above all, any program you choose should be easy to use, so that your child's first experience with the computer will be successful and rewarding. The following lists, published in High/Scope Educational Research Foundation's computer newsletter, *Key Notes,* include a diversity of software that is developmentally appropriate for preschoolers.

Ten Starter Programs for Apple Computers*

1. Muppetville (Sunburst)

2. Kid's Stuff (Stone and Associates)

3. Counting Critters (MECC)

4. Number Farm (DLM)

5. Estimation (Lawrence Hall of Science) (concepts of time)

6. Size and Logic (Hartley)

7. Colors and Shapes (Hartley) (both seriation and classification)

8. Dr. Seuss Fix-Up the Mix-Up Puzzler (CBS)

9. Mask Parade (Springboard) (children create masks, hats, and other dress-up items on the computer screen. They can then print them on paper to be colored and worn)

10. Color Me (Mindscape)
* *Courtesy of the High/Scope Educational Research Foundation.*

Ten Starter Programs for IBM Computers*

1. Kindercomp (Spinnaker)

2. My ABC's (Paperback Software)

3. Kid's Stuff (Stone and Associates)

4. Number Farm (DLM)

5. Pockets Goes to the Carnival (World Book)

6. Pockets Goes on a Picnic (World Book)

7. Pockets Leads the Parade (World Book)

8. Pockets Goes on Vacation (World Book)

9. Pockets and Her New Sneakers (World Book)

10. Mask Parade (Springboard)
* *Courtesy of the High/Scope Educational Research Foundation.*

Commodore C/64/C64C/128*

1. Muppet Learning Keys (Spinnaker)

2. Early Games (Springboard)

3. Mask Parade (Springboard)

4. Stickeybear ABC (Weekly Reader)

5. Stickeybear Opposites (Weekly Reader)

6. Number Farm (DLM)

7. Ducks Ahoy (CBS)

8. Dr. Seuss Fix-Up the Mix-Up Puzzler (CBS)

9. Odd One Out (Sunburst)

10. Color Me (Mindscape)

* Courtesy of the High/Scope Educational Research Foundation.

6. *Choose hardware that will grow with your child.* The very inexpensive computers you often find in toy stores are not necessarily the smartest choice. Once your child tires of the limited software available for these stripped-down models, you're stuck adding memory and peripherals that will add up to a more costly (and less versatile) machine than you would have had by buying a more powerful computer in the first place. Besides, they usually feature cassette drives, which make starting up and error correction a time-consuming process that may turn off your budding computer jock soon after she's turned on the machine. If you're considering buying a computer for yourself anyway—say, if you or your spouse would like word-processing or spreadsheet capability—consider one with a disk drive, 64K of memory, and preferably a color monitor (because many preschool programs depend on color for their menu choices and games).

For safety's sake, check that the computer is more or less childproof. On some models, high voltages are present at locations easily accessible to small fingers. Instead of a traditional keyboard, you might consider a membrane keyboard designed for kids (such as the Muppet Learning Keys) and made of wipe-clean plastic with pressure-sensitive keys. These are appealing to kids because they're colorful and easy to read. And parents like them because they're not inclined to go up in smoke after the first apple-juice spill.

As of this writing, your child will have the widest software selection if you choose either an Apple II, Commodore 64/128, or IBM model. Any of these will not only run a wide variety of the better preschool software, but will be useful later on when your child starts school. *I have yet to speak to a computer learning expert who recommends investing in such a pricey machine for a mere preschooler, however;* if you don't think the whole family will put it to good use, find out whether your public library has a computer for children's use and sign your kid up.

7. *Sit down with your child at the computer.* Preschool software has a long way to go before it becomes self-explanatory. And just as your child needs you to read and explain a storybook, she requires an adult interpreter to guide her through a program.

At one preschool using LOGO, teachers help children bridge the gap between the computer world and their daily lives by having them narrate stories about the graphics they create. At home or in the public library, try to get your child talking about what she's seen on the screen. If she has conceptual difficulties with the movement on the monitor—for example, understanding how a line on a paint program moves left or right—bring her back to the world of three-dimensional objects and her own body. Suggest she stand up and imagine that *she's* the line. Just as your child's love of books deepens through the experience of sharing them with the adults she is closest to, her confidence at the computer will grow with your encouragement.

In the long run, that's probably the best you can hope for your child if you decide to introduce her to computers at this age: confidence. If she discovers that she can *play* at a computer now, she's unlikely to be intimidated later on in school when the time comes to *work* at one. There's no reason to believe that the computer is an indispensable teacher of subject matter that can produce children who are better readers or walking calculators; a normal child will learn to read and add whether or not she spends any time at a keyboard. Feeling comfortable with computers, acquiring a rudimentary sense that *people* control *them* and not vice versa—these are worthy goals for a child, and they can be achieved in any of the ways described in this chapter. As always, however, the most important thing is what your child learns about *herself.* If she looks forward to time spent at the computer because it provides opportunities to practice her growing skills, to explore, to be rewarded with a feeling of mastery, and to share her accomplishments with a caring adult, then it's *one* way to help bolster her self-esteem and love of learning.

Who Really Wants a Superbaby, Anyway?

This is about acknowledging that your child . . . is a Separate Person whose development in many areas may have nothing to do with you. Regardless of nature and nurture, regardless of the long line of athletes, artists, or preachers in your family, regardless of years of loving exposure to your politics, your music, or your work, your children are likely to break out in unidentifiable talents all their own.
—Letty Cottin Pogrebin, "What Wonders Kids Are,"
Ms. magazine, March 1988

TODAY, MORE THAN EVER before, raising a child is a great leap into the unknown. Parents of past centuries took it on faith that a child's well-being and growth to adulthood were in God's hands, even though many children in fact did not survive infancy. In today's secular world, where nothing is left to nature and our ability to control our own destinies is the measure of our self-worth, child-rearing has become a test for parents. Do we know all the latest research on every conceivable area of development?

Can we translate it into age-appropriate coaching that will secure our child's upwardly mobile place in society?

How terrifying. No wonder parents are looking for a head start anywhere they can find it. In California there's even a Prenatal University, where fathers-to-be are trained to instruct their five-month-old fetuses to "kick Mommy," and third-trimester unborn babies are drilled on the words *pat, rub, squeeze, shake, stroke,* and *tap.* Parents who are more technology-minded can buy a Pregophone that attaches by suction cup to an expectant mother's belly so that they can provide baby with verbal stimulation before birth. (Whatever happened to closing your eyes and imagining? Or to the days when Dad talked to his unborn child via Mom's bulging belly button?)

Amusing though the superbaby approach sometimes sounds on paper, in practice it is hurtful and saddening—not only to children but to parents as well. The growth, the curiosity, and even the mistakes that were once cause for laughter and awe are now matters of high "scientific" seriousness. I am reminded of a scene from *Confessions of Zeno* (1930), a comic novel by the Triestine author Italo Svevo. In it the protagonist is sitting in a café with a hypochondriacal old schoolmate who explains in minute anatomical detail the process of walking:

> He told me . . . that when one is walking rapidly each step takes no more than half a second, and in that half second no fewer than fifty-four muscles are set in motion. I listened in bewilderment. I at once directed my attention to my legs. . . . I could not of course distinguish all . . . fifty-four parts, but I discovered something terrifically complicated which seemed to get out of order [as soon as] I began thinking about it.
>
> I limped as I left the cafe, and for several days afterwards walking became a burden to me and even caused me a certain amount of pain. I felt as if the whole machine needed oiling. All the muscles seemed to grate together whenever one moved.

Like overanalyzed walking, child-rearing becomes painful and grating when we get so bogged down in the details of cognitive and motor development that we are unable to relate to our kids spontaneously. To make matters worse, the more we buy into the pseudoscientific approach promoted in misguided manuals and advertisements, the less we trust our own instincts. Instead of taking joy in the closeness we feel as we lovingly watch our child develop in his own special way, we are forever holding up a milestone chart to measure his progress. All those amazing aspects of his personality that can't be quantified—his goofy sense of humor, his tenderness, his resilience—are lost by the wayside. In the process of trying to simplify reality for educational purposes, as Valerie Polakow Suransky points out in *The Erosion of Childhood* (1982), the child is reduced beyond recognition: "All that the child is, or was, became observable, measurable, and, therefore, capable of experimentation and control in the interests of schooling the young."

Why would anyone consider it preferable to crush kids' individuality at such a tender age by subjecting them to rigid institutional learning? They are bound to miss out on something precious. As Jonathan Kozol puts it rather pessimistically in *The Night Is Dark and I Am Far from Home* (1975), "School is the ether of our lives by now: the first emaciation along the surgical road that qualifies the young to be effective citizens."

The Exciting Possibilities

When we dare to see our children as the gloriously complicated little people that they truly are, then we are presented with a much more enticing opportunity than superbaby training. We can actually *listen* to them. We can hear their highly original theories on the laws of nature. We can hold out a steadying hand as, of their own volition, they leap into new worlds of knowledge, from riding a trike, to trying new breakfast cereals, to counting the gravel in the driveway.

Does this sound too chaotic to produce any results? Well,

consider for a moment how much our children actually *do* learn without direct instruction from us. As the Soviet scholar and poet Kornei Chukovsky wrote in his classic book *From Two to Five* (1968),

> It is frightening to think what an enormous number of grammatical forms are poured over the poor head of the young child. And he, as if it were nothing at all, adjusts to all this chaos, constantly sorting out into rubrics the disorderly elements of the words he hears, without noticing, as he does this, his gigantic effort. If an adult had to master so many grammatical rules within so short a time, his head would surely burst—a mass of rules mastered so lightly and so freely by the two-year-old 'linguist.' The labor he thus performs at this age is astonishing enough, but even more amazing and unparalleled is the ease with which he does it. . . . In truth, the young child is the hardest mental toiler on our planet. Fortunately, he does not even suspect this.

The beauty of early childhood learning is that there is no need to force it. Given the freedom to explore his world, the child will ask questions, questions, and more questions. Each piece of new information provided by a responsive adult will help him put together the puzzle of his universe. Rather than being put through his paces by a worksheet or program with an externally imposed set of questions, he grows in whatever direction his own imagination and understanding take him. In the natural ebb and flow between his desire to learn and the power of his imagination lies the richness of child-directed learning. "To a certain extent curiosity comes naturally to the young, but its development depends upon a growing awareness of the power of well-ordered questions to expose secrets," writes Neil Postman in *The Disappearance Of Childhood* (1982). "The world of the known and the not yet known is bridged by wonderment."

Deprived of this richness of experience, a child can acquire all the "basic skills" under the sun and fail to develop the maturity and imagination required to really understand the world. No matter how young he is when he learns to read, his ability to make sense of a text will depend to an enormous extent on his emotional development and life experience. Were you forced to read Tolstoy in high school? I was, and although I could obviously comprehend the words, they never really sank in. The books were bewildering, boring, and wordy. And yet now that I'm in my thirties, how profound and eloquent they seem! Is this because I'm a more "skillful" reader—that I know more multisyllabic words, for example—than I was in high school? Obviously not. It's because the intervening years have given me a perspective on life, and an understanding of some of its joys and sorrows. These are lessons that can't be taught.

What Do Our Kids Really Need?

"Never let success hide its emptiness from you, achievement its nothingness, toil its desolation," writes Dag Hammarskjöld in *Markings* (1964). Deep in our hearts, we all *know* this. During the past year alone, the newspapers have been filled with reports of broken lives—on Wall Street, in Hollywood, in national politics, and among wealthy TV evangelists. Chemical addiction, marital strife, teen pregnancy, and suicide seem to plague our society's most materially successful families. Every one hundred minutes, according to the Centers for Disease Control, a young American commits suicide. Anxiety is epidemic, as the television executive Barbara Gordon wrote in her harrowing autobiography *I'm Dancing As Fast As I Can* (1979):

> I was a lucky lady, lucky to be able to merge my politics, my passion for the First Amendment, my private self, with my career. . . . But if I was so happy, why did that creeping terror come over me every time I tried to go out for lunch? Screw it, it's manageable, I told myself. . . . I've got a super job, a super man, a wonderful life—and anxiety. Who doesn't? I just didn't want to make a career of it.

It should be obvious that the critical task facing us as parents is to attend to our children's emotional and spiritual well-being. Teaching them to recognize Beethoven flashcards and print the letter *E* seems trivial by comparison. Must we *choose* between the two approaches? I think so. You can give your child the message that he is loved for his achievements, or you can let him know he is loved for the unique human being that he is. It's an either/or proposition.

What Do We All Need?

We live in a precarious world. The American citizen of the late twentieth century who picks up the newspaper over breakfast is greeted by the threat of nuclear annihilation, a weakening economy, a rapidly growing homeless population, racism, sexism, third-world starvation, religious strife, street violence, and the list goes on. In the eyes of many, there is little cause for optimism about the future. In fact, many adults of our generation are refusing to have children on the grounds that today's world simply isn't a safe place to raise them. Those of us who are parents have a very personal stake in the future of humankind. As you rock your baby to sleep each night, can you look down at his face and even grasp the possibility that he may never grow up to learn what it means to fall in love, or to hold a child in his own arms? Sad to say, these are not mere philosophical questions, as Jonathan Schell points out in *The Fate of the Earth* (1982):

> To the obligation to honor life is now added the sanction that if we fail in our obligation life will actually be taken away from us, individually and collectively. Each of us will die, and as we die we will see the world around us dying. Such imponderables as the sum of human life, the integrity of the terrestrial creation, and the meaning of time, of history, and of the development of life on earth, which were once left to contemplation and spiritual understanding, are now at stake in the political realm and demand a political

response from every person. As political actors, we must, like the contemplatives before us, delve to the bottom of the world, and, Atlas-like, we must take the world on our shoulders.

As parents, we have the awesome task of helping shape the leaders of tomorrow's world. And considering the time and energy so many of us are spending on superbaby training, it is not at all inappropriate to ask whether the future of our planet depends on our children's abilities to count from one to ten at age two, or to zap alphabet letters on a computer screen at three. Given enough love, guidance, and freedom to explore, the preschool years are a time when children learn to play together peaceably, to think creatively, and to feel good about themselves and the universe. What lessons could possibly be more important?